out of the pine woven
fabric steps the sun

out of the pine woven
fabric steps the sun

J A Y S N O D G R A S S
2015

For Kristine

out of the pine woven
fabric steps the sun

Journey beneath, I found a road into a city, arboreal crease, crescent. There were marks lining the way, indicating me on. I went, spherical into the air, into the map in the air, in outer-space practicing the imprint of these, this city flash, in the air, mapped, made of trees.

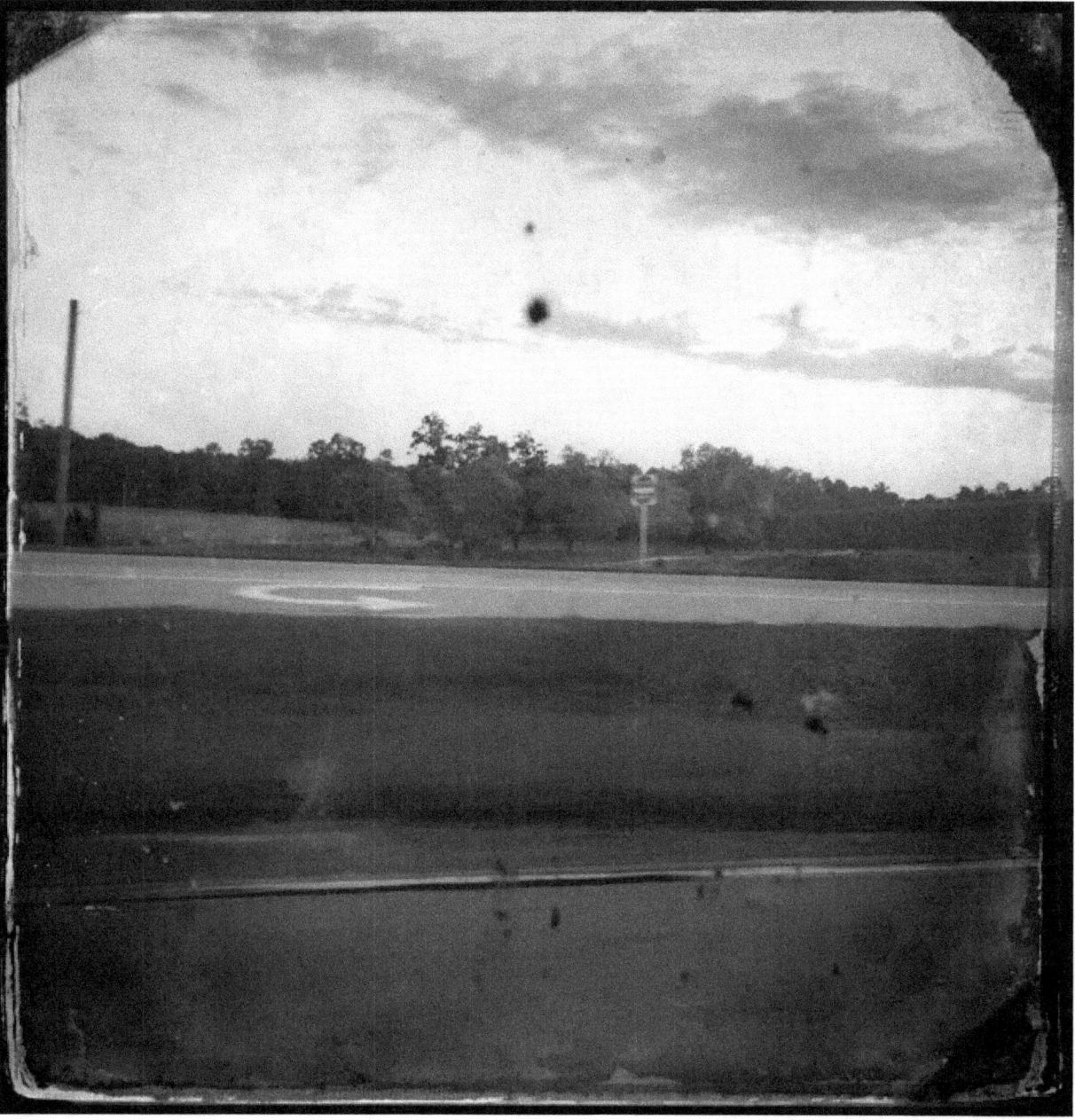

Out of the pine woven curtain steps the sun. Trucks are reawakened, alive to their moving. The undergrowth is a bramble and decay. The racing by ignores it purposefully inured to resurrection.

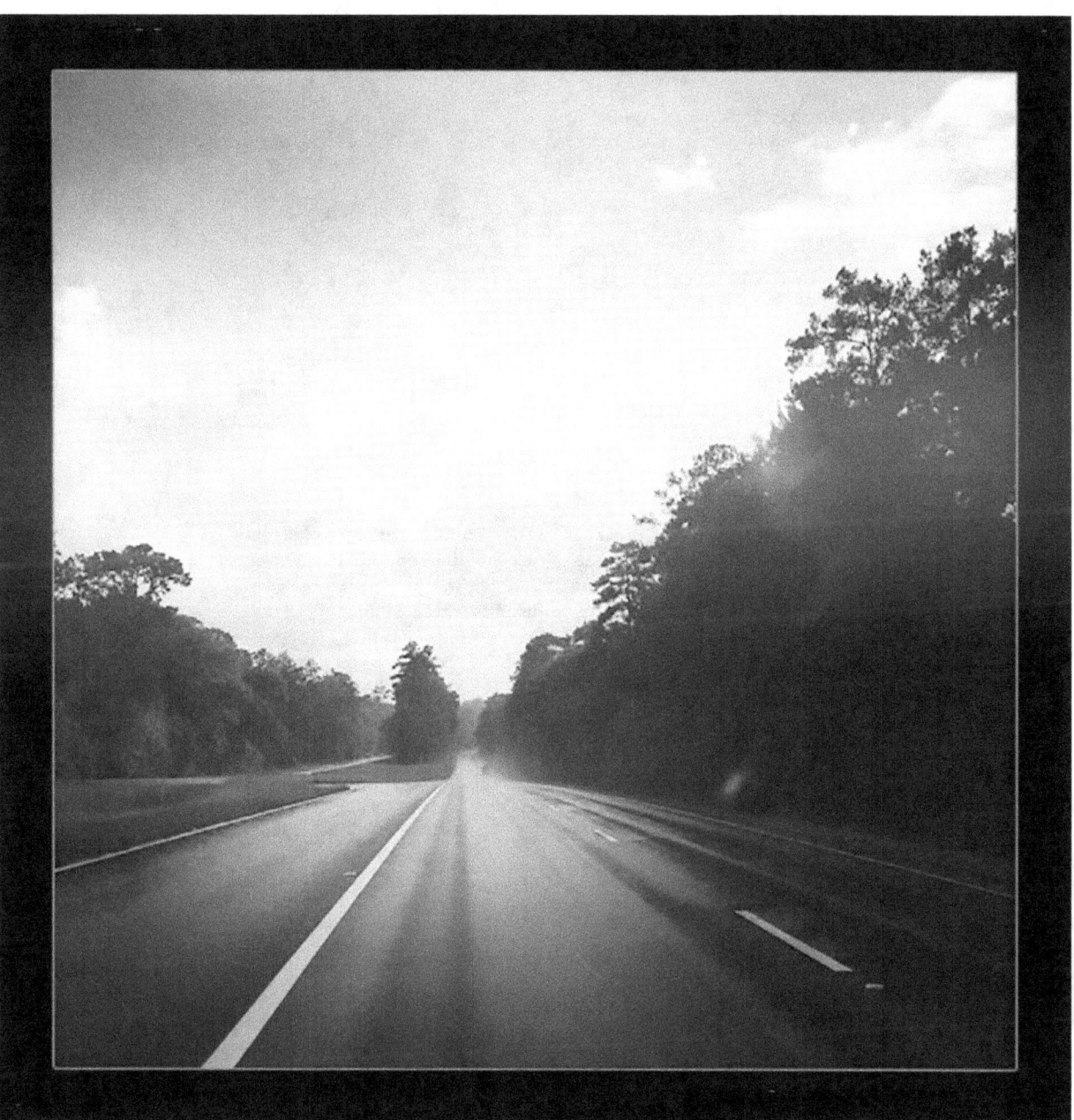

I dream, I cannot dream, I cannot stand, I cannot feel. I am resistance, I am a sneeze, I am holding on, holding down, back. Putting together up and down into one category. Perhaps I am underwater, ender sky, these moments. Cloud.

The forest is severed for this road. Engine burn as sap sweat, the face of night in searing, the Spanish Moss coming away in clumps like Chemo hair. Wet, wet, the rain tries to erase the road. The hands upon the wheel are pure. Cleaned of ghosts. Aluminum by hours.

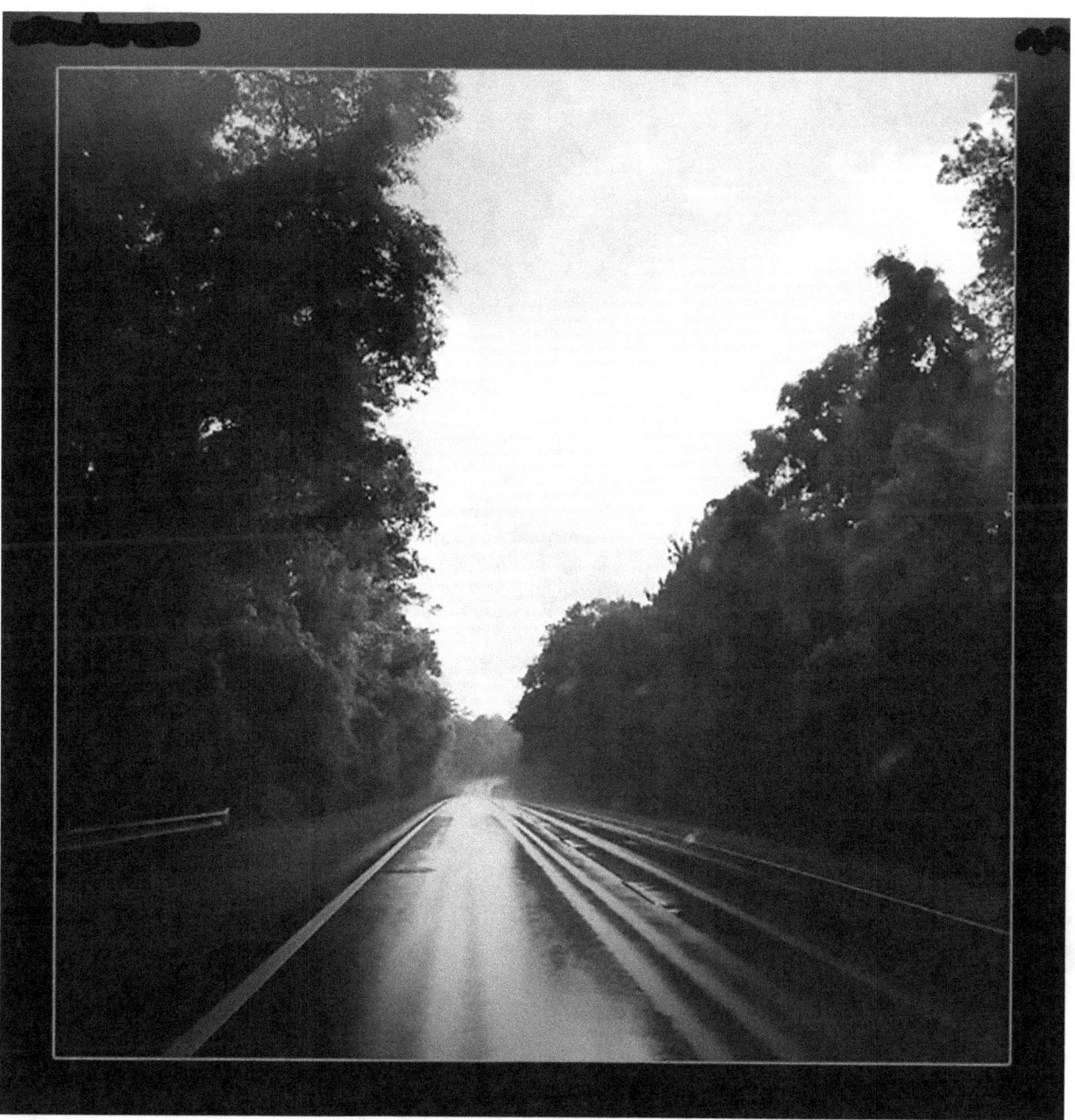

It's long, been long, too long for a dead man. The shifting eye turns only with the moon, glimmer, naked a street lamp. Moist flesh turning to alcohol, grape dreams in finger tips. Hair turn gray, white hair in the gray crumbling pine straw, graying with grease, oils dumped at the bumps in the road. O how long is the night.

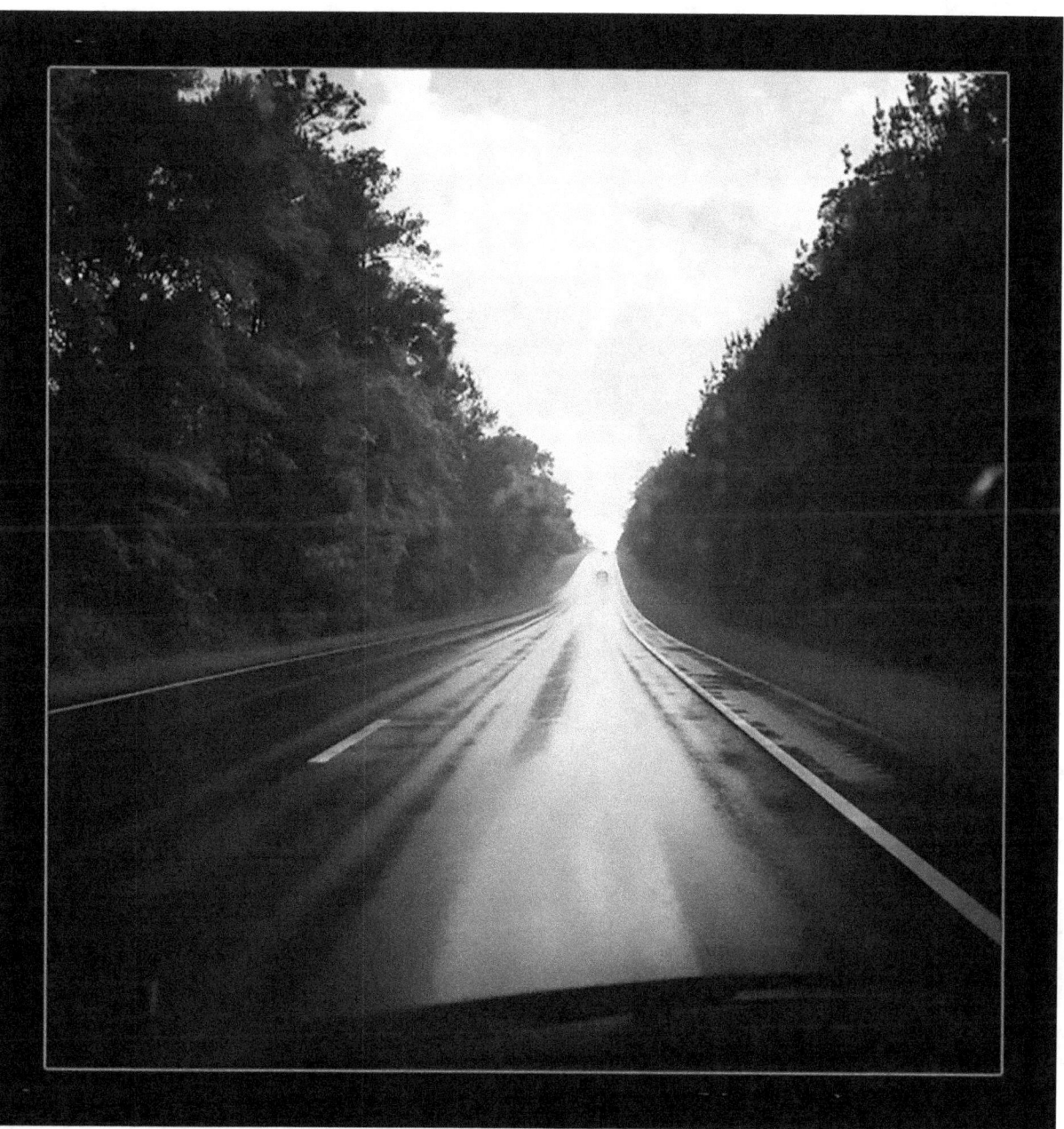

Everywhere, riches are pouring out. Pouring into. There is danger on these roads. The skies are all diamonds. It's a wonder no one's noticed. It is risky to even be here. Someone might notice.

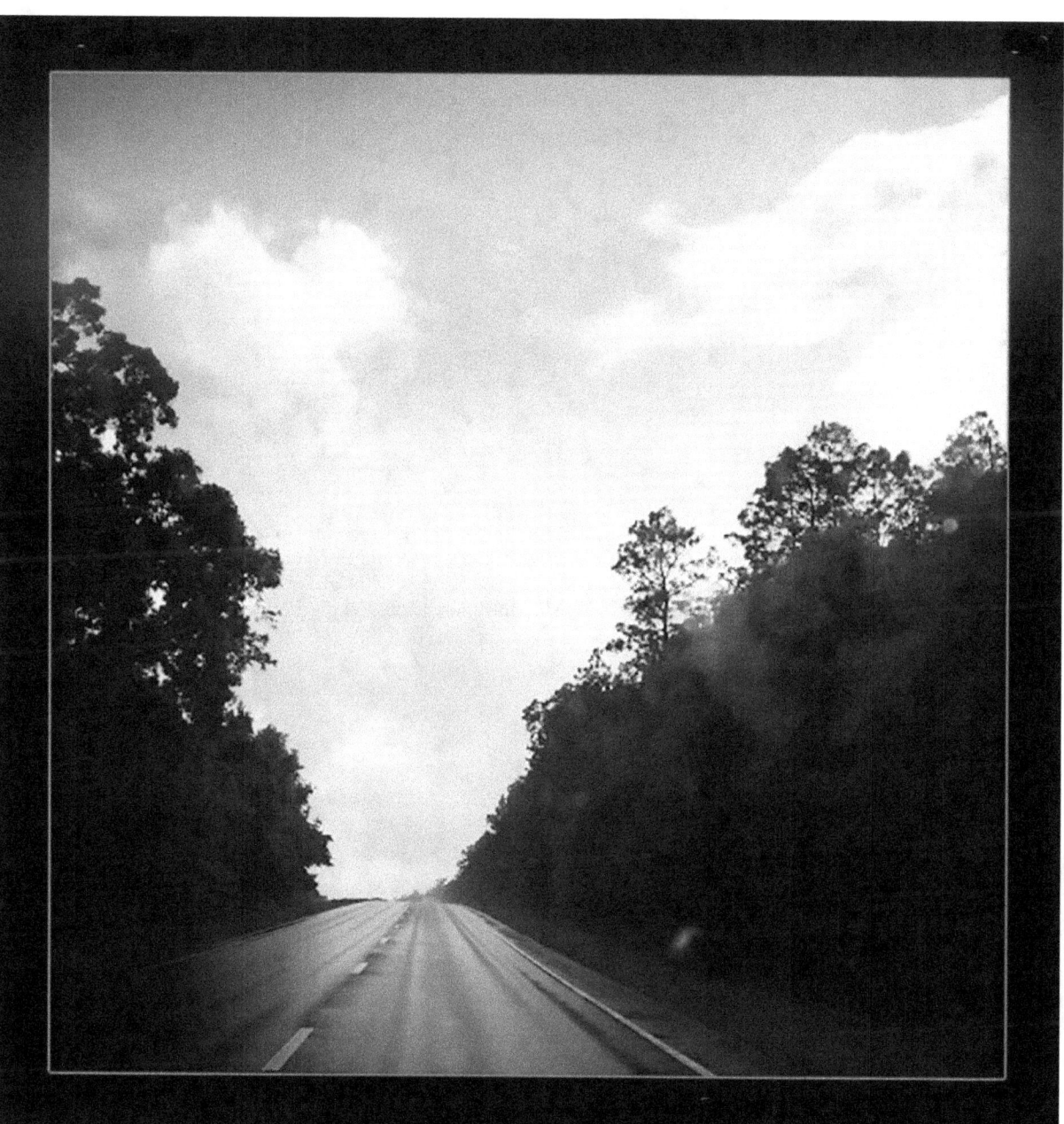

We both knew there was a border to the world. I found that edge in your pocket, among the tangled notes and coinage. Your sign is a creased ax, your star is the woodcutter. Cut in glass, he is deranged from travel. There is only mound and sky. Another.

Here is a seam, rich, dark, to the underworld. Where there is a body, there is passage. Moving. Feet stoppage. I am above you looking; you are down looking up at the movie screen. It is a sky and you're in the age of black and white and meaning. A cloud like a tendril of smoke connects your eye to my ashtray.

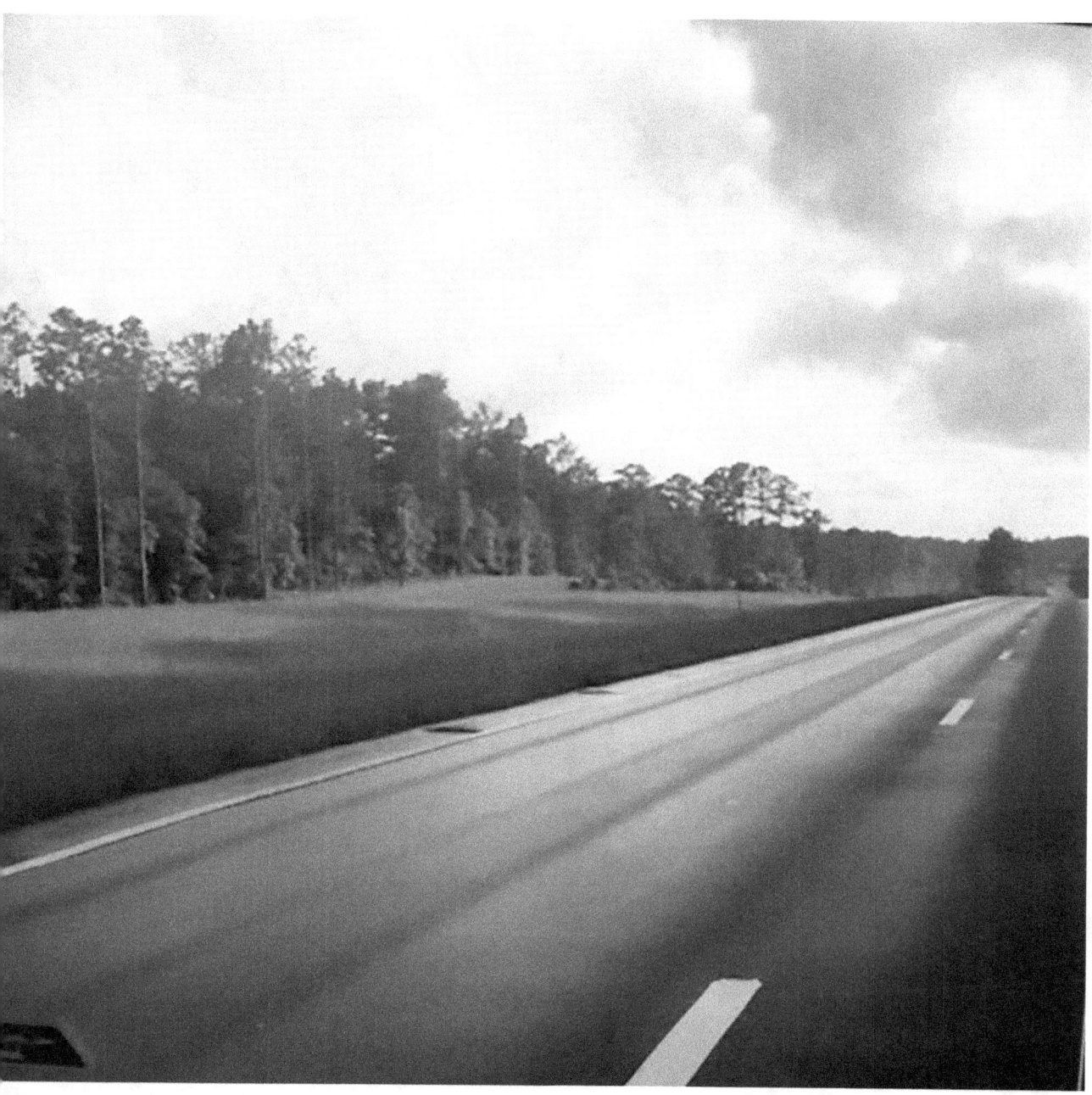

You may travel four years on the back bone, sitter, sky grader, but it may be in your interest to learn to change your appearance, as many travelers do before entering dining establishments or romantic relationships. It is a trick of the sky to change its appearance from one day to the next and still be a lover, providing the substance of movement, water and drowning.

Crawl from the machine into the sunlight, into the horizon skirted. Smear tar on my legs and road rash, knee scrape on canvass, gutters and canvass. I strangled the far hill into another horizon, white line rope, I loved her thousand fingers, thousand souls. Glitch of Angel filled.

Driving, childlike, the shadows increase to cover your eyes, you resist. Listen for the word of it, I am sad about this, the clouds carrying what they do, spilling it on us, and we are greedy, contemptible.

Now the belly, the bell, ringing out the sound in the war, the war in the cloud, the clipping of hair and snap of scissors. The road is a ribbon. It is a dark ribbon of hair on a carved wooden doll. The face is not a human face, it might be a horse, or another whole body shrunk to fit the face. Hips and breasts and eyes.

I'm lying out, asleep but driving, driven, sky mesmerized, white line drunk. Yellow wild flowers blooming over manure, great serpents of manure claiming again the forsaken gardens, paradise, rush and jasmine, and blue bonnets towering over nations of ants.

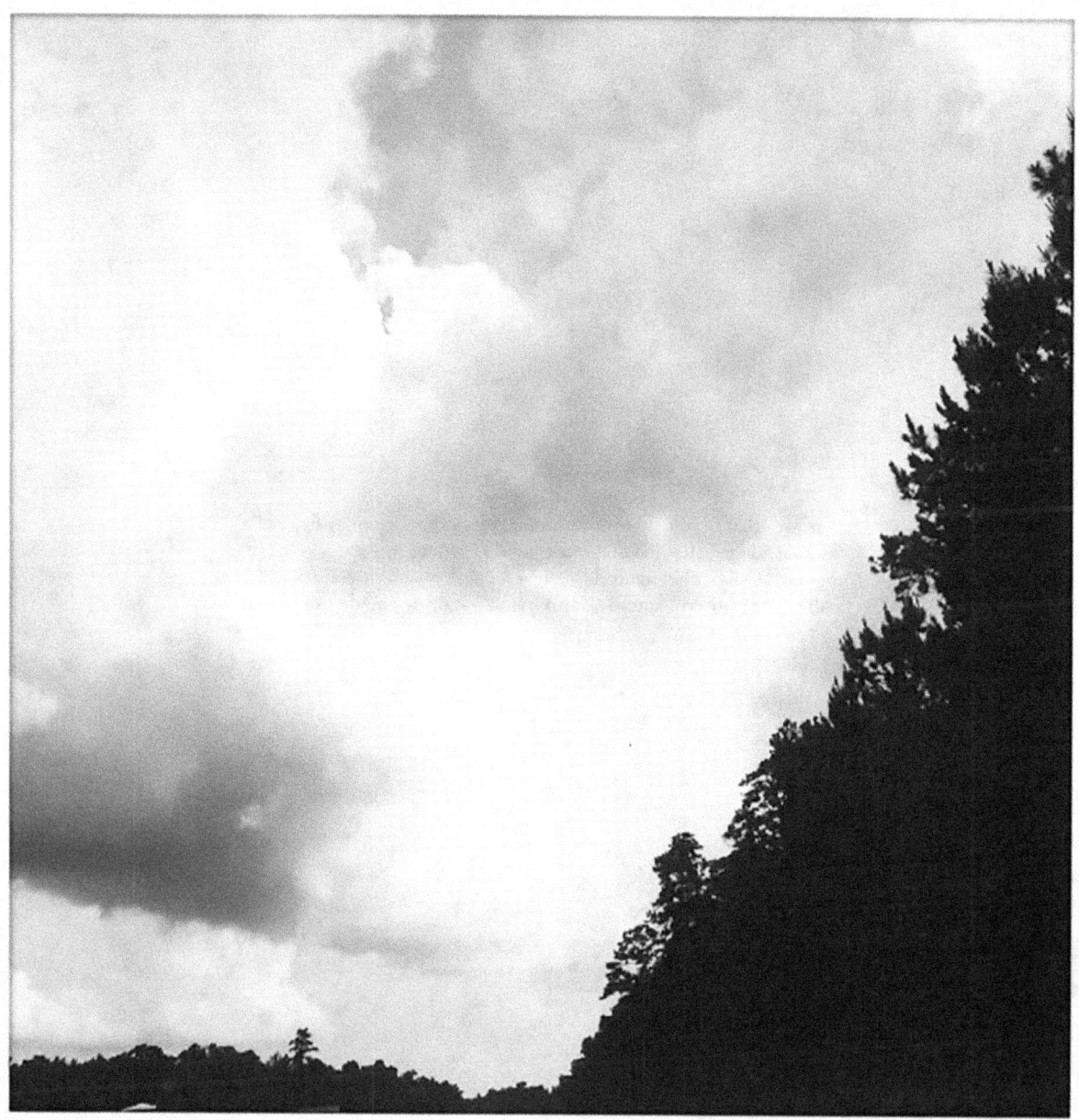

Know that you cannot overcome the resonating, the animal that calls in the dark forest, where only eyes move, hover. Only the sound can escape, also, uncoiling like saliva, a liquid sound from your mouth made of eyes.

Torment, hot like the engine, fever. Like other illnesses, carried along in the blood, in gasoline, in canisters to far lands, country mad. How regular, how priced common.

There are many faces revealed in the side mirror or the brightened face of the truning car, caught in the beams, sudden and crazed. But the road is flat, the creature of a bulldozer's dream. The signature of mankind, the tracing of eternity's face, tamped into a moment of surprised recognition.

Flowers fall, to be dead, to be alive again around a cage. A car is a cage and flower is a cage of looking. The body is called a chassis, it is hidden like underwear, and a woman wears the height of the tree tops like a gown.

The mercury gallows, silver fast, it slips away up the high ceiling in your apartment. In your dream cage. The cellar is gripping and silent, which is how you want it, sort of. But you don't want to be frustrated by the poisons in your fish, in your heart, and so you evacuate into a future, into a distance.

The ceiling is painted to resemble the sky, lay me down within it, city, sky tomb. How that city is made of folded paper and wire, and even a little breath and spit. How it wants to understand. How we want it all the time. Itching like a body, to touch.

Breath against the window each hour, a mark and then drying over. Small crusts are forming from the patterns. Ancient grooves as from a volcano, millennium since, gardened over by my ancestors and eventually turned into a road fringed with garbage and snakes. A throat of calloused dreams. Shreds of a plastic bag streaming in a cold breath like snakes.

I can't hear the silence in my heart. It's beating. rage in the shade. The paper thin walls of my car shine in new wax and insect blood, love insect, love. I give it back but as always, my trespass is too late. I've smashed everything delicate with my passage, just by passing though.

Throw it in to the sea, the sky, and watch it bloom with bloating, with ink from the octopus escaping the growing cloud. Escape the necessary confusion, scrub and scrub and scrub until even the faces are removed.

I can see you have come this way to collect some remnants. You are a harvester of the tempest, the ligature of landscapes you weave into a tapestry to hang above your dinner table. But the missing element is a boiling current, hard to discern in the sky's opacity. You may miss it's ubiquity, it is contained in the brush of grass upon the wind, a culmination of charged particles.

Dream of the future of air, full of men and women driving and being passengers, being in the shape of companion, shapes only, and voices to carry on the purpose of motion, of night, night's revolution of prayers like the stars to a tree. Rotation.

Hold at bay the revelation of the secret. Holding that secret away requires the effort of television watching, serene, reclined effort, like the forced luxury of a fallow field, waiting for the harrow. My heart, my love, misplaced the road in/out, I probe.

The road transforms your soul, preparing, alchemical steel tables to lay out the language upon. Sweet body, sweet flower, sweet dissected purpose. Listen like a cucumber to the salad, to the plate, to the vinegar, to the mouth. Play dead, Bacteria, play dead.

The dark forest balks against the sun. A grumbling semi, and a young man's ambition fires like cannon into the sweet quiet. Detritus, left out, over man and woman yellowed skin as far as the moon's kiss. The guard rail resists your doom, resists the slid into ice, into skins of eternity.

It hurts, for real. In me and you, the television relay, playing itself over and over in your memory for the sake of our genes, the future generations at their song. Turns out the song is a jingle to sell, but not to sell dignity. That's unfounded.

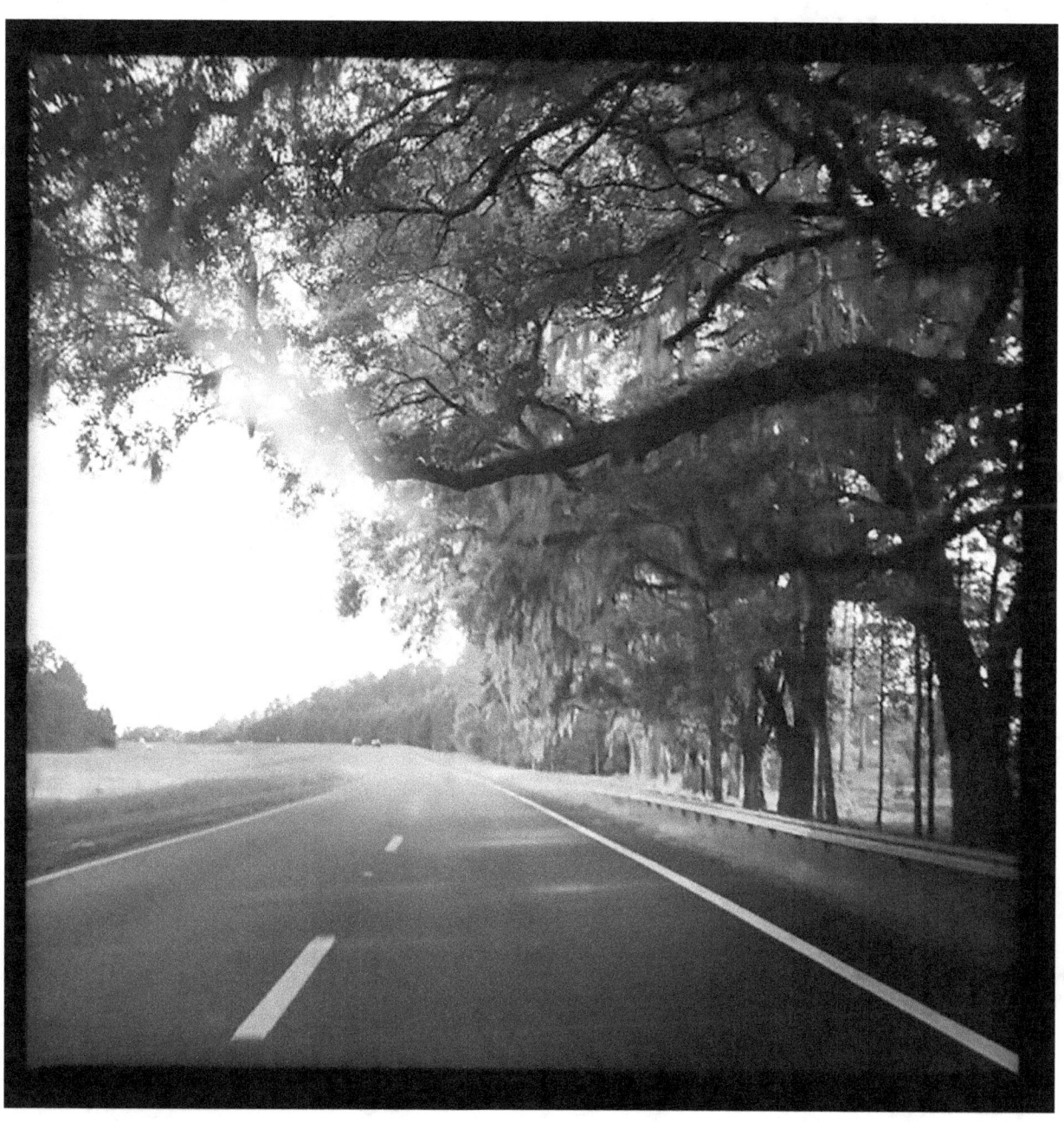

Can you remember? Just beyond these gates, paradise doesn't say anything. She is quite and still. She is still and sky and clear. Bloom gowned, she sticks out her tongue to taste the road. It's a tracking technique that humans do to find their way back into paradise.

God inflates the lung as sands with waters, blossoming they grow like a breeze, like a wave pusher, into a sand mouth into a cloud into a rumpus into a storm into a hurricane into beech, render it memories and landscape and horizons.

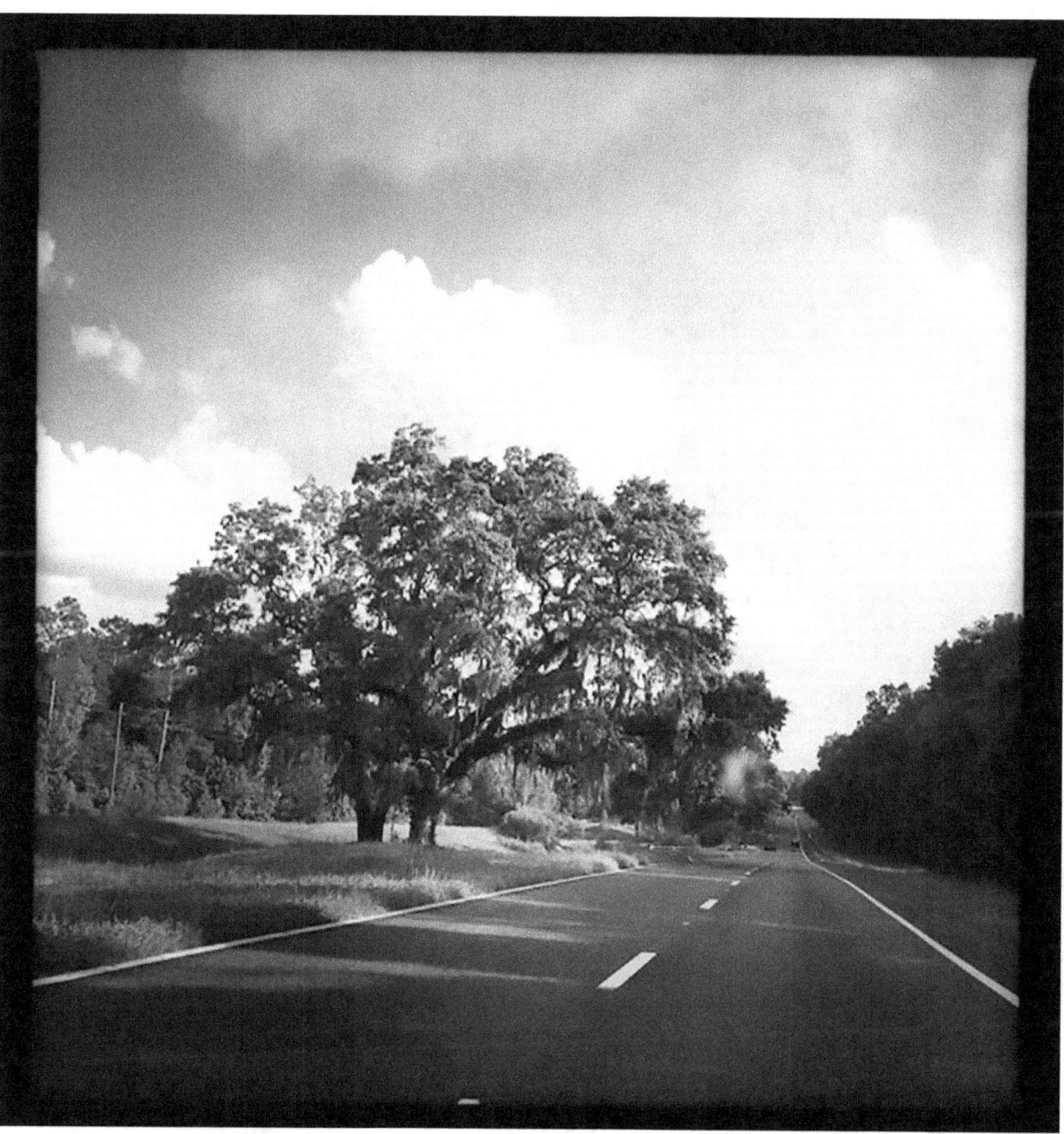

Often the sky is mosaic shards of tile beneath the worshipper's feet, making little cuts. It's not the patterns of the shards that are important, though specialist will study them and reproduce them, but the way they pattern the cuts in the walker's foot, into the child, the celebrant, inductee, mule, sacrifice, goat.

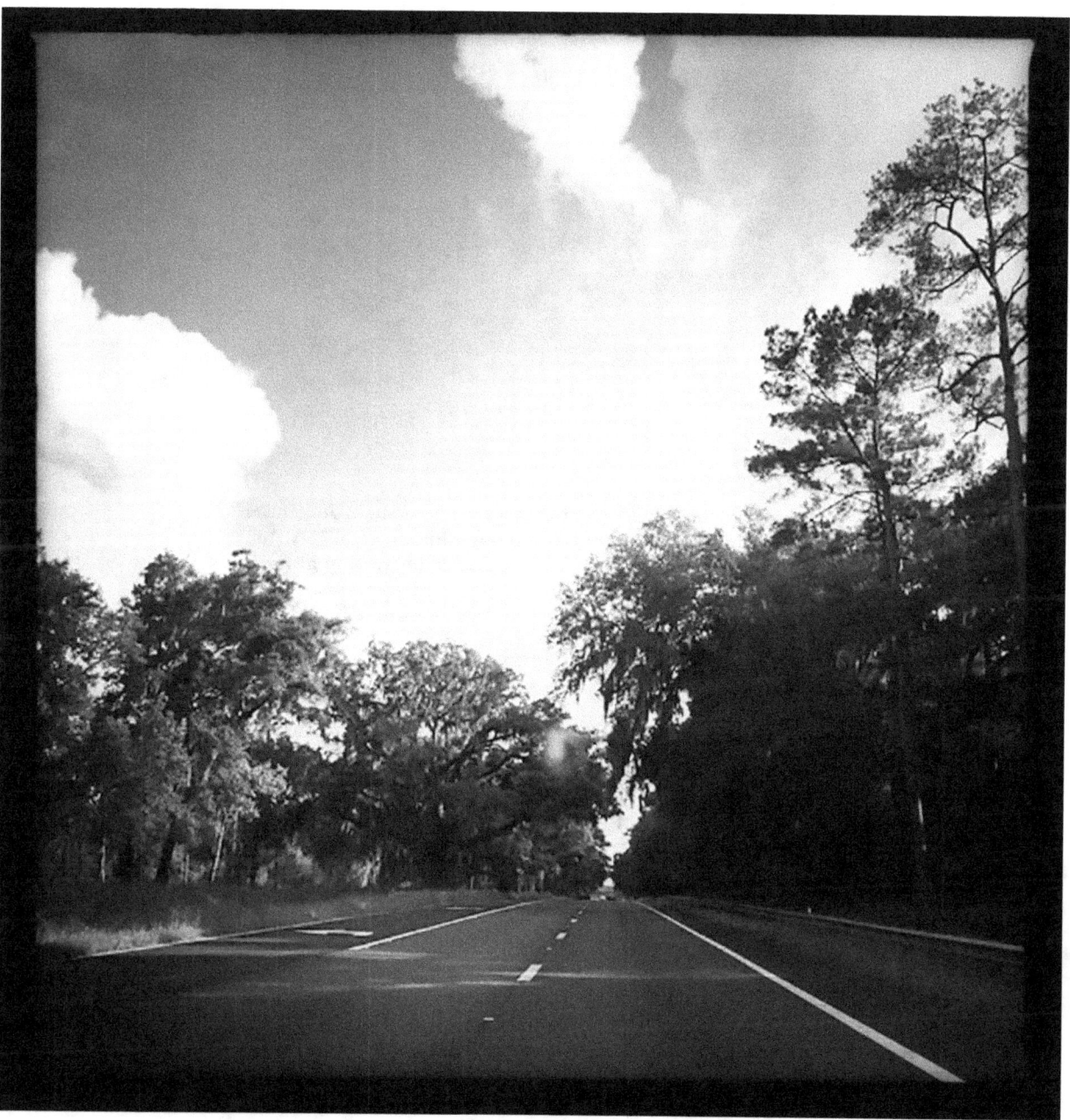

I can turn the compartment of my car into a study. Illuminate the studied manuscript of the highway with my headlights. You may lean over my shoulder, hear the crunch of gravel in history's road making. Be compressed in the mind, until the ballast of your thoughts are tamped into a precise level. Come, walk with me.

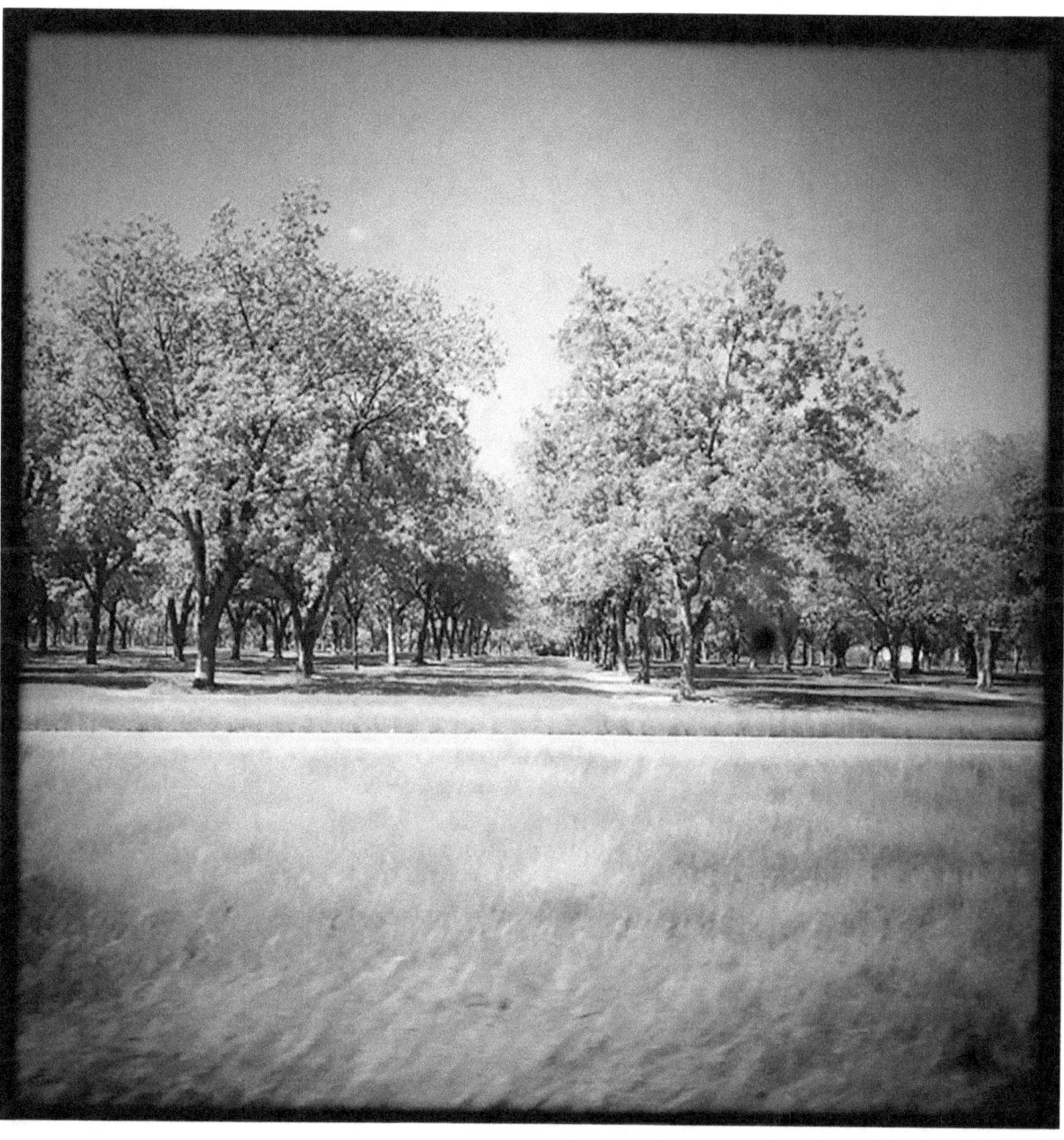

The shadows have eyes that laugh at us, passing cups, deep unfortunate cups. The piston, fired upon pulls a rod which turns a wheel. Speechless with the violence of it. The power of violence is how undeniable it is, especially when it is sudden. If you are prepared for it, then it is mute, or derived from love.

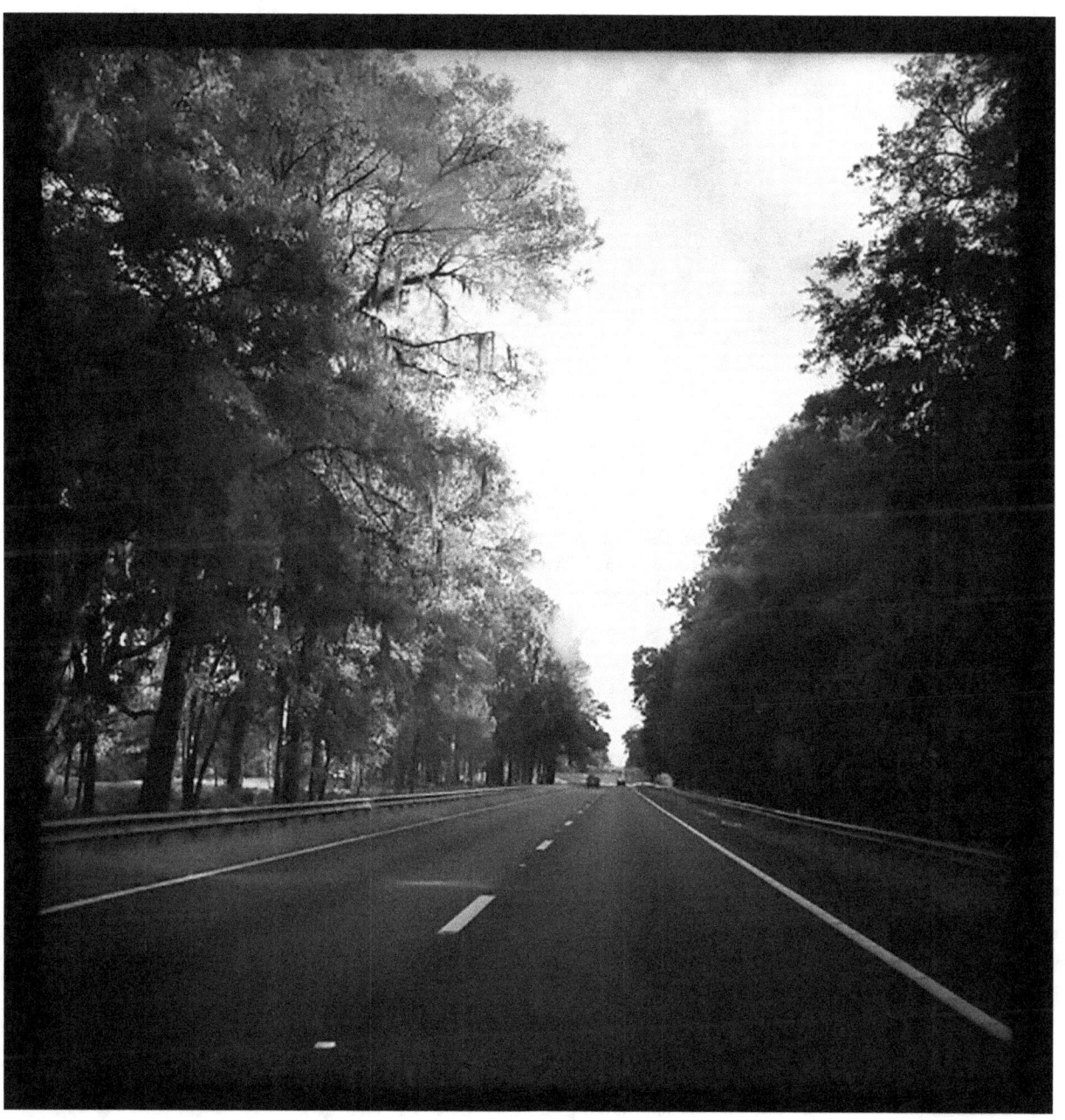

The sky is relentless now, and what of it. Its suffering is also present and remarkable as though documented in a film for television no one will watch. Binge on suffering, sky. Fill it until it is perforated.

Every cloud is a signature, proof, the average of what you can say. You can, for instance, address a pawn broker as though you weren't interested in the armoire, its indecipherable detail and missing pegs. No one believes in legs, nor inadequacy. This is a test, you may assume, about grammar. You have failed. At speaking.

At the least of my shadow, there, I appear most beside the god who has expelled me. Photos of us on Facebook put evidence in to the heart of the damned. We were, despite the callouses, affordable in our silences. In love.

Open the road of what happened and scrape something out. It may be thick and smell of benzene and fish. There it is, emanatiing from between the earth's deep palms pressed in prayer or rage. Thin strands of petroleum spun into fabric, so thin they are like glass, translucent. Peer inside like it's a paper weight, the weight of things put to use, the willing servant standing upright, black coat and white collar neat like a road, and solid.

Listen, the gas station has parking places, slots to lean in, rest and purr and count your earnings. Spend it on a million candy bars while the teams of trucks sail on, distant and close, tossed away.

Beyond the bright sky, the stars are set still, waiting to return their consumption. Tall glasses on the bar, crenelated peripheries. No one bought any of your limeade. So clever and insecure. I'm going to buy your old weaving, let the staring public know it can survive.

Plants turn toward the sun by some design, the streaking object thrown by some hand, shot through with digital light as though from an alarm clock, the red kind, bright. I've been in the shops, peering into the eyes of ceramic owls and cats. No sign of my mother. I flip through post cards in plastic sleeves; they are protected from being touched by me. When the lights go out they can return their gowns to the hook and go home for the evening.

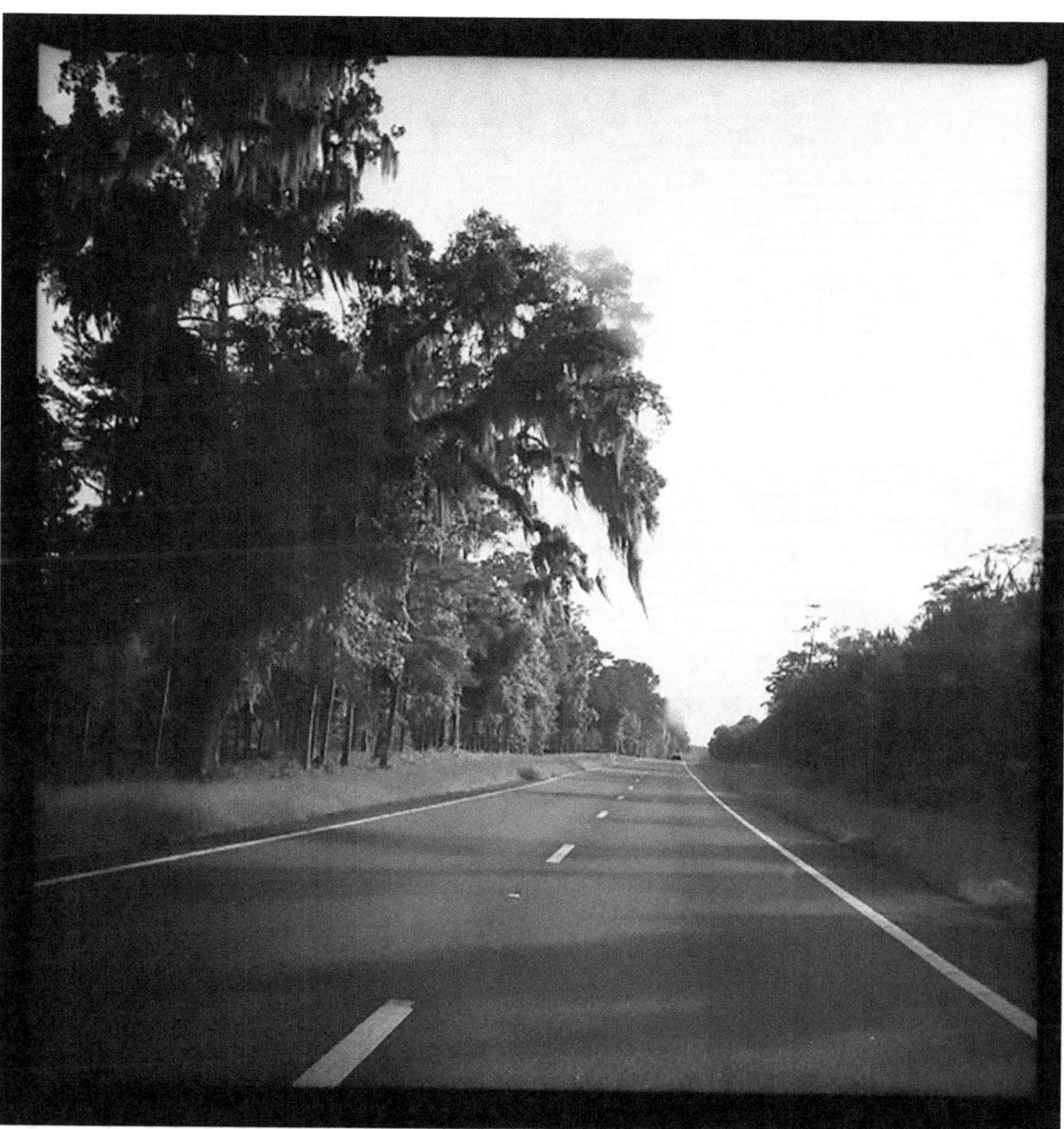

There are coins in the slot, in the ashtray, in the seat spaces beneath us all. The swerve comes on when you reach away, turning lidless eyes and searching for a coin upon the floor. The toll booth's apron awaits.

Sometimes I drive without thought, animated by another spirit, habit, un-remembering, presence of the god who patiently kneads my skin until I die of comfort. This process may take 80 years but I am steady like a yeast in dry weather. And I pulse as though in a strong wind. No one suspects there is joy in these shadows.

Against rolling, against thickness, against the will, world and pride, turn your knuckle boor, turn out a measure of soil and place stones as deep as a man, as deep as the procession of stars to the north. Build your temple so that it looks like the far temple, beneath a radius of trees, so that the stars seem to turn in service to it.

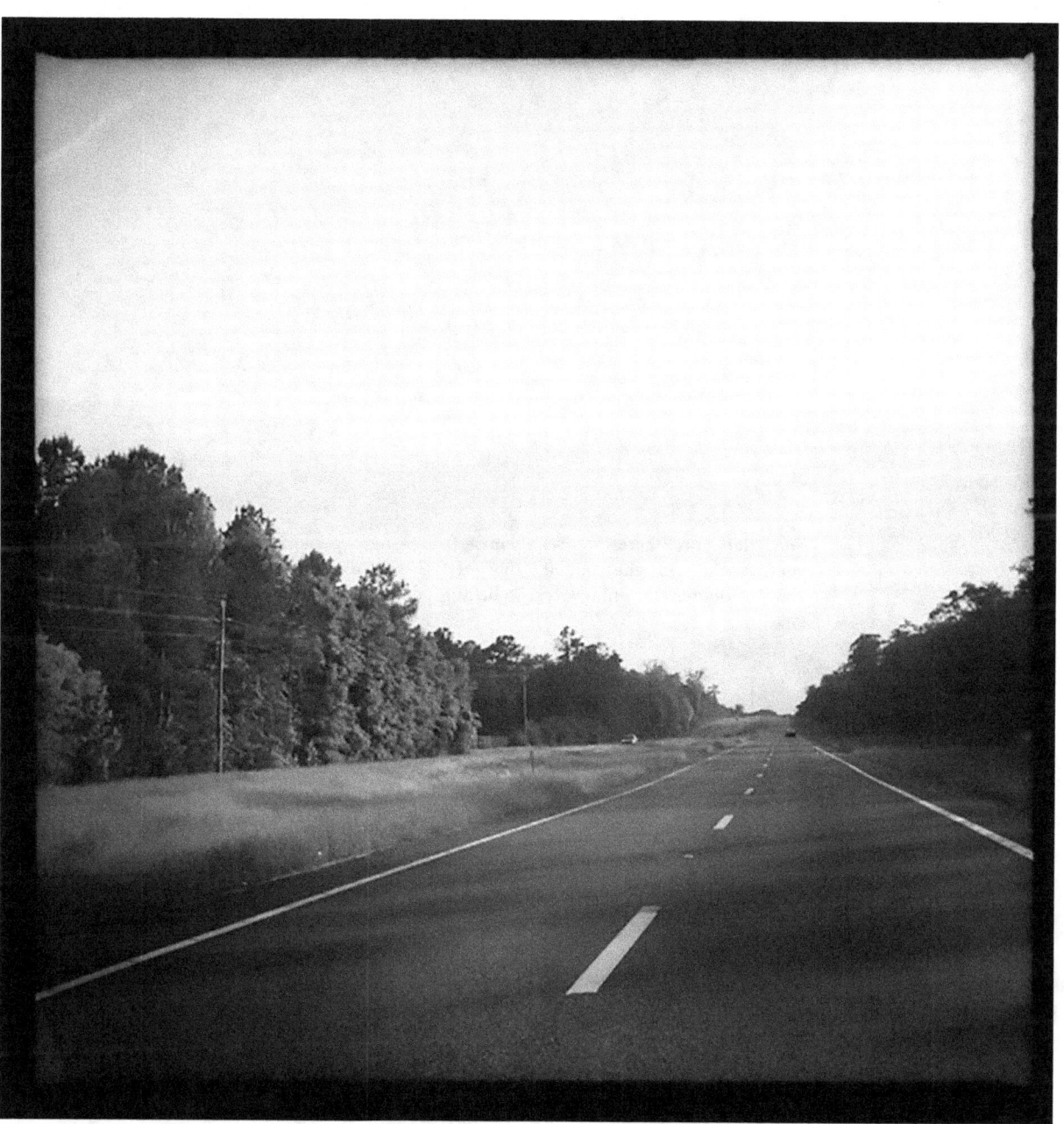

You, too, are here to see yourself looking, memorizing your clothes in the mirror, the wet clouds drooping off your shoulder. Humid, sick, clicking deformed whispers.

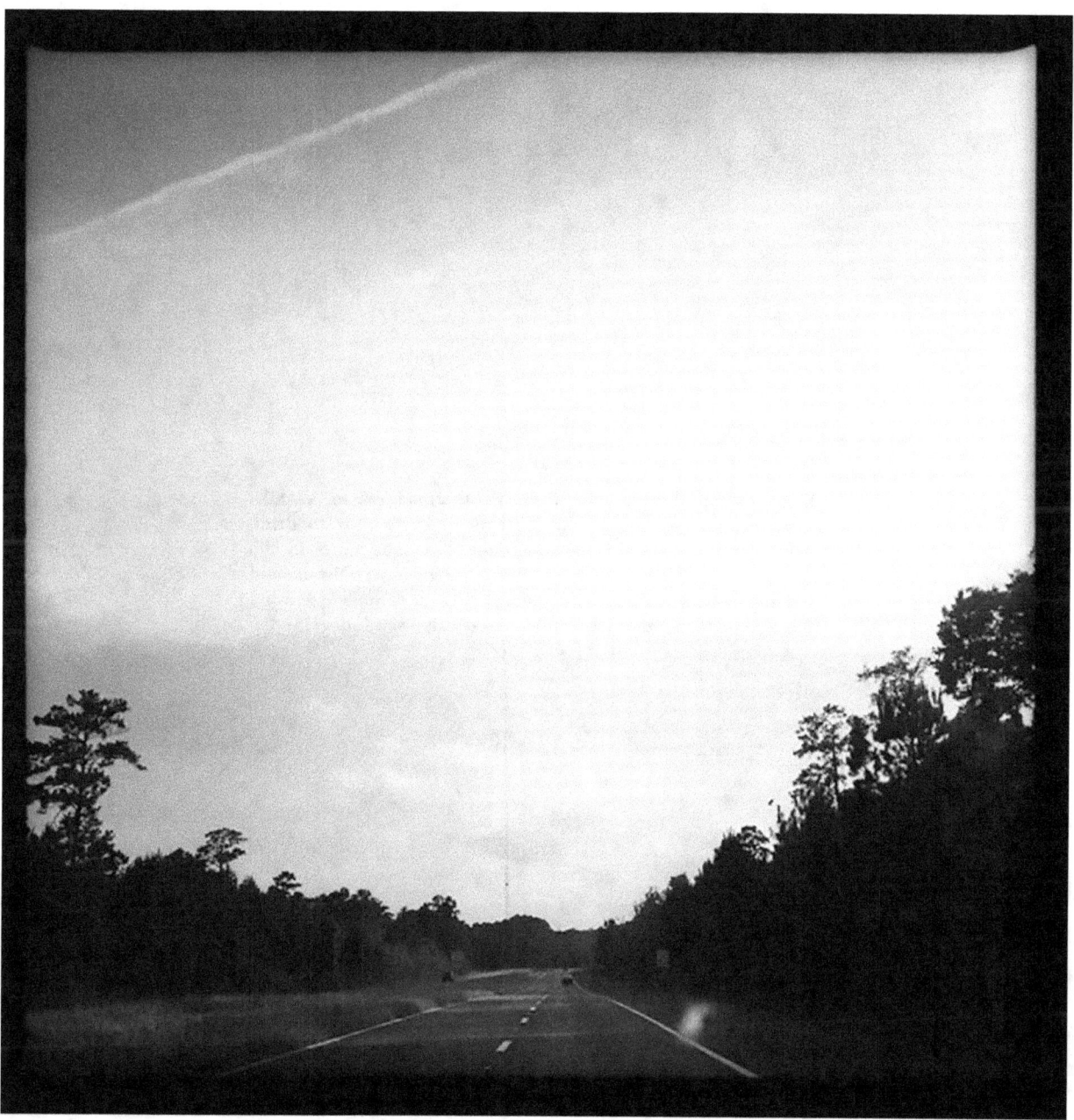

There is a sound in the wind that stills the madness, for a while. Some people use this to shop, others find the time to drink and recover. I'm in the bending light, like long grass in the field. Recoverable but still too distant to register. Distant and obscure. Like late afternoon gloom on a dark polished wood floor. Something that absorbs sadness like sand does water.

There is a language here, but it doesn't mean anything, doesn't mean praise or shame. Doesn't mean harrow the insects from your life and sheets, doesn't mean judge me as a child. There is a language in the trees, the bonnets of sun scattering through in barcodes, codes, odes of laser light. Beam in to me soft wood, pulp my eyes into light. Discover

Child, what have you done with all the money that spilled from the overturned banktruck? The coins like snow, the weeping feathers of bank notes, twirling in the twilight?

The highway leads from one set of circumstances to another. It is distinguished by its generosity, by its volume of unremarkable carcasses. The pavement is a cycle. The methods of scraping things flat is cyclical, the means of polish are rotation. The wheel is how we return. The horizon is the same horizon as it ever was. Because you can come back to who you were before you left, we call homecoming sacred. When you are transformed by a fissure in the road, you may come home but you can never return. Stars through the glass.

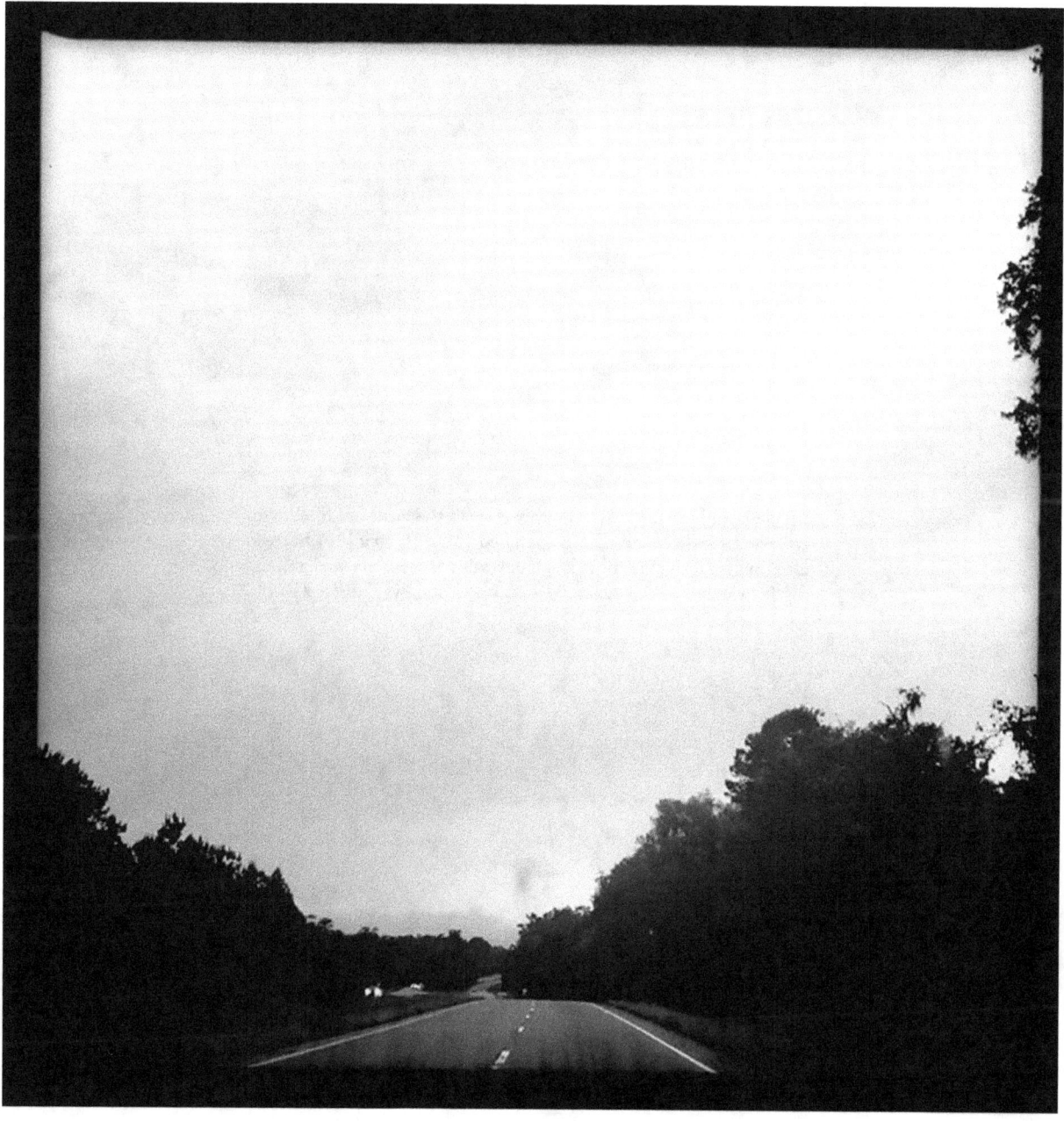

I have been here for years, the carcasses of the birds are filled with collected plastic ends. The dispatched thirst in wrinkled bottles, elegant as elderly skin. Blue labels corroded to veins in which miners dig for the ore of the ocean. Water, water and everything a brink.

The trees, as you pass, are gesturing frantically that this is not the cure. The blooming jasmine, radiator steam, what the British call the "bonnet", all around you crumpling. The space you are invading does not provide solutions. It is not the kidney or the knee that is broken, diseased, enraptured. The trees are indicating that you are on the long path. If a driver were to notice, they might turn to the passenger and remark how windy it was.

There is the dangerous curve, the shadowless turn of the head, the receding origin over every sound within your mouth. There is the dark center of your eye, the point of recess this road disappears into, singularity, on and on, cumulous observed and blessed.

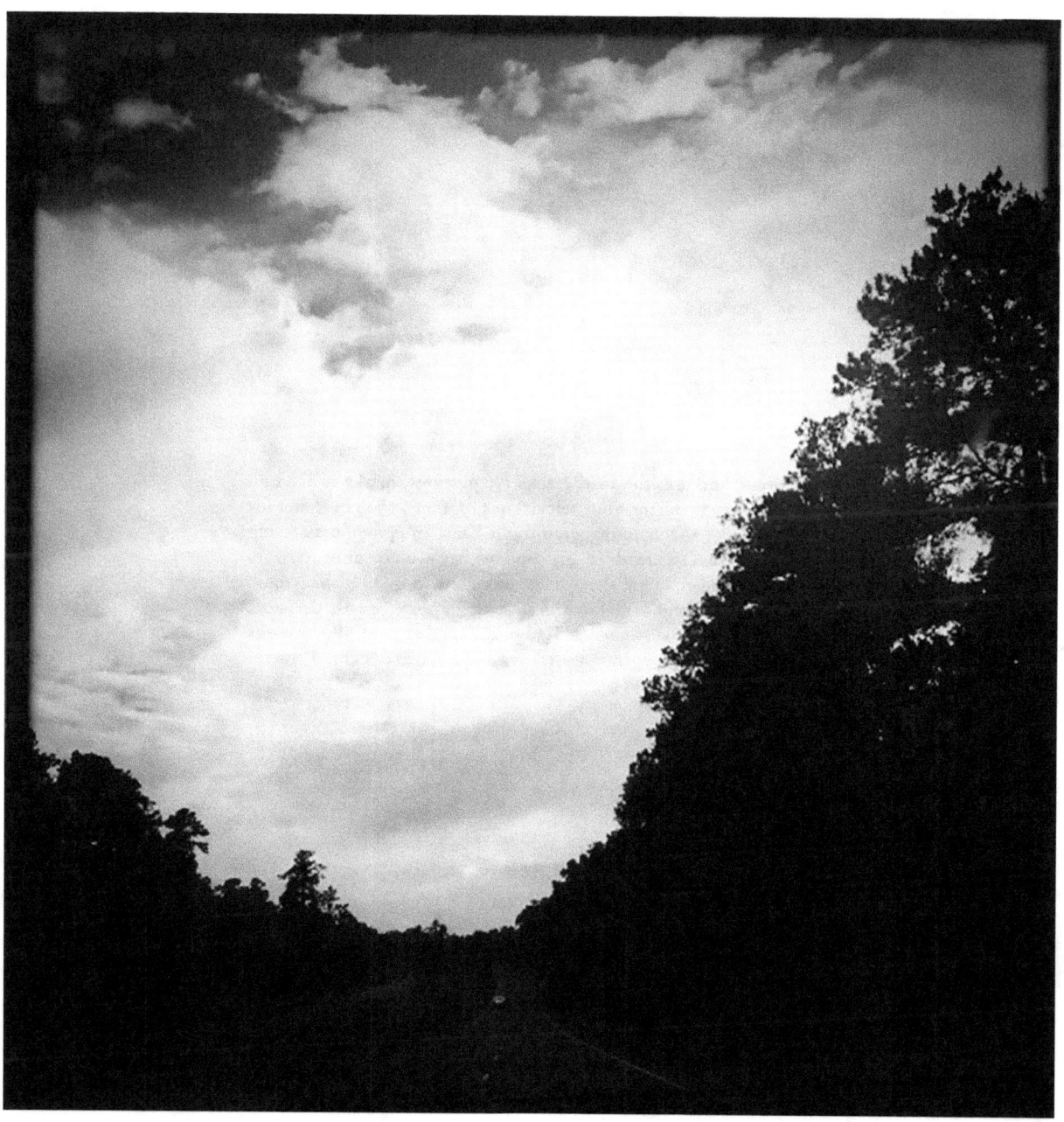

Varicose horizon, the road cracks are gestures, marks to read on the face, your mirror, your television programs, choices that a fox might make about timing. Last night I saw an opossum assessing when to cross the road. It surprised me because the only opossum I see on the road are dead ones, attended to by minister crows. But this one was still the animation of choice, crisis, decision. The fast food customer looking up at the food illustrations back lit by tube lights, aghast with dazzle and befuddlement.

There is an unraveling in the road, it reveals what I am not able to communicate because I was not properly equipped, just as I cannot see the colors that the butterfly can see when it zeroes in on the Zephyr lily, wind botched but beautiful beyond my eye's ability to reproach. I suffer because I am blind to the radiating patterns built in to asphalt, yellow, white, blister oil-bloom. I go on, an oblivious servant.

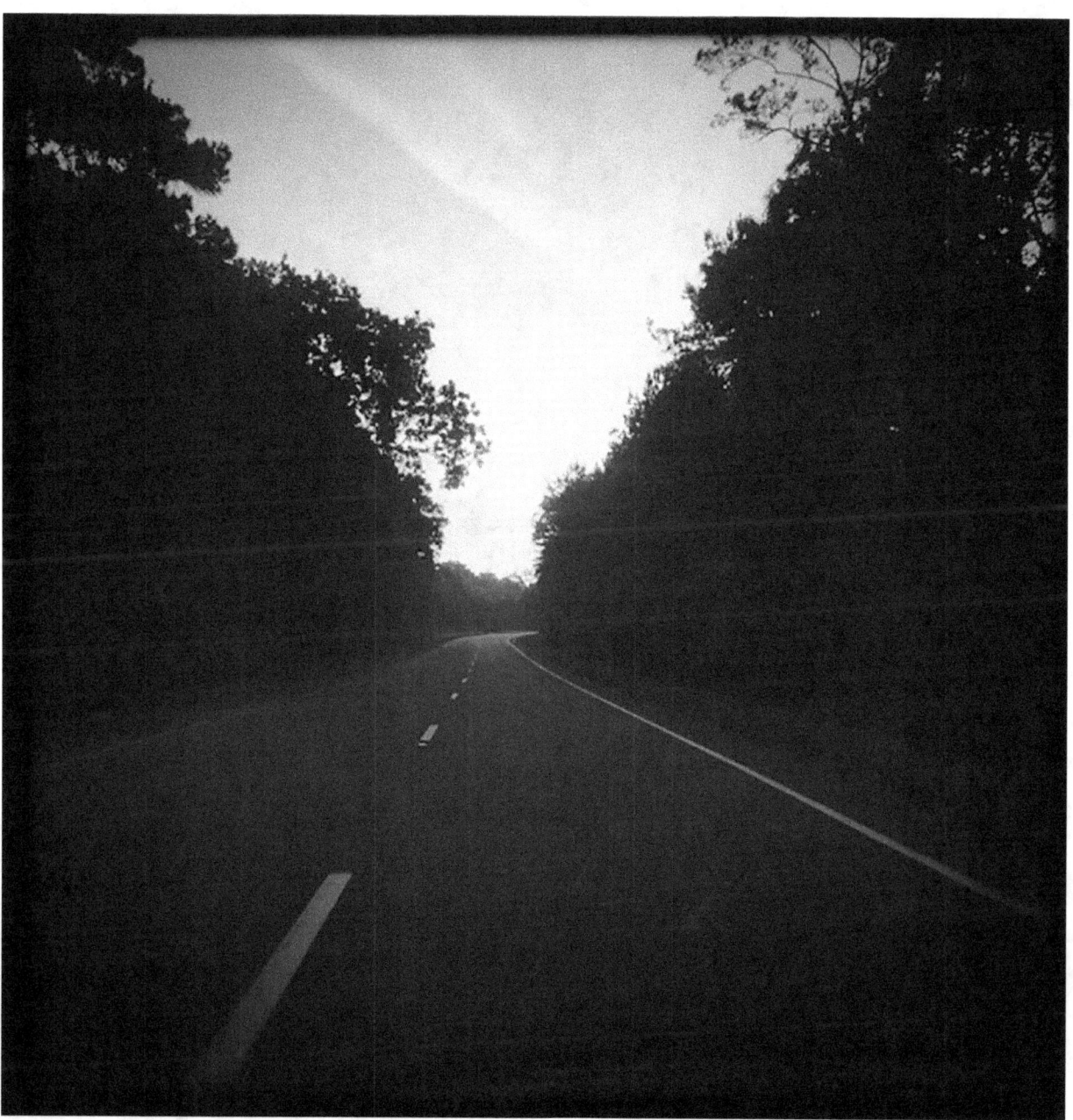

In this turn the final moments are preserved in sunlight, the final moments of a million car wrecks, held still in the beams between the loblolly and trash pines. Like children held in the arms, like men cutting eyes, there are flickers of notice and then, generations bear on.

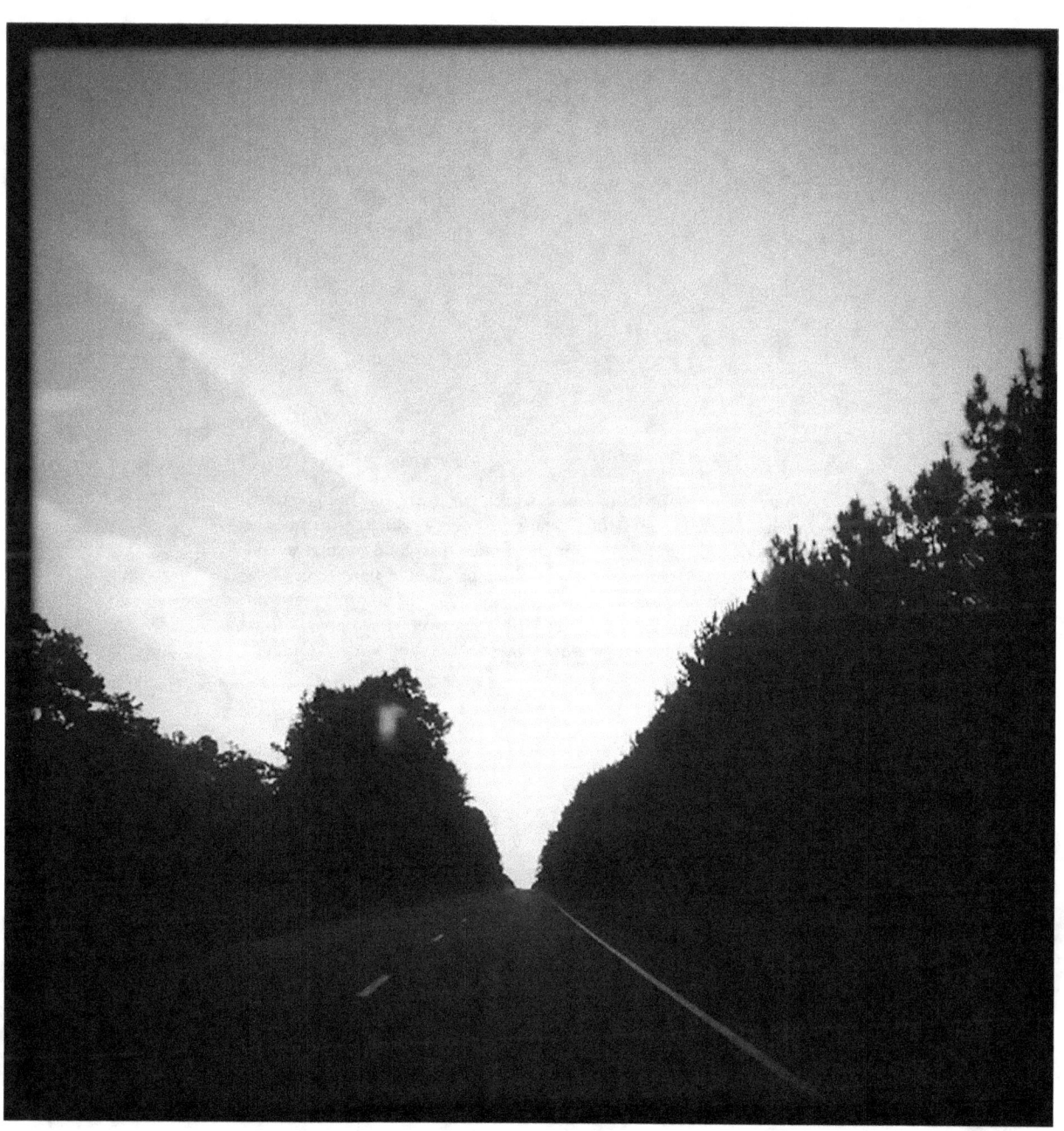

There is a purpose to your travel, to turn out and return, again. To repeat and thus create an energy which, with greater frequency generates a magnetic field. This field insulates you from external radiation. The yelling of distant voices receding into a kind of peace. The path is smoothed by an excavator, an odd euphemism for when the birds pick over your bones. Thus the road is generated by your body to be your body. Terminal.

There are birds etched along the highway, they draw your thoughts away, plucking out your driving eyes. They attend their duties. autopsying the armadillo for evidence of its murder. We have all murdered it. The highway is sunk three feet down for every grave.

There is a shadow in the sky as though by explosion made, and glass and scarred aluminum. The god of calamity is getting fat, you can tell by how she loosens her timing belt, how her rubber is split everywhere.

I am this far out to sea. I must keep going now, to turn back is as much a mystery as to go on. But it's not the sea, it is the road. Still murky black though and bearing up submerged mystery. An almost infinite unknown quantity of life.

Some drivers escape the chord of home. Some circles are tightened by the cities they live in. Men and women talking walks, driving to the grocery, look out over the far tree tops and think of escape. Just as the chords are jerked and the heads are turned back into the cars, into the door ways, into the dark hollows of your eyes.

How far into the peripheral do you have to go find the wild wheat, the cotton shores. Perhaps I am just a fish in current, darting desperately in and out of shadow and shoal, avoiding tractor trailers and truck stops. Searching for a purpose, to eat and continue.

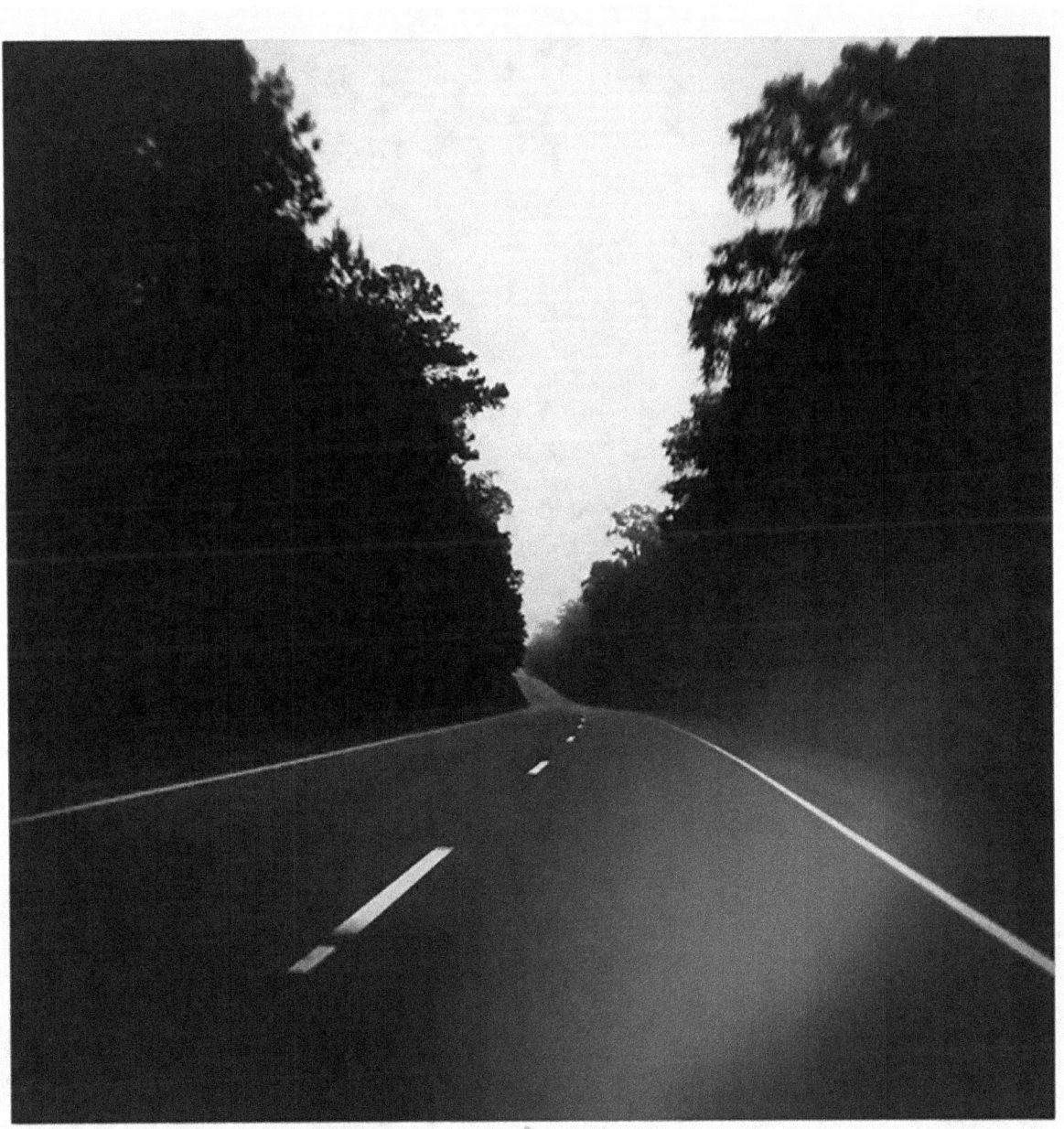

In the flashing lights, the accidental alarms, overhead and burning
. The tree's embarrassment where the squirrels chit and shame,
are illuminated in high beams, urgent like a spaceship moving
away, moving through the dark and lighting things differently
for once, if you notice. The quick light on the leaves helps us
in the dark to know there is a limit, an edge. The grooves cut
in the side of the road rumble with impending chaos, thunder.
Awake! Awake! They also illustrate the borders of things,

In the realm of the sun, the shadow is servant. Just as the children grow into darkness, so your name lives a little in the shadow beneath you, beneath your carriage. There is always a shadow under your car. And your needs are inadmissible. The fingers of resistance, the silencing gestures stand guard at our lips, covering.

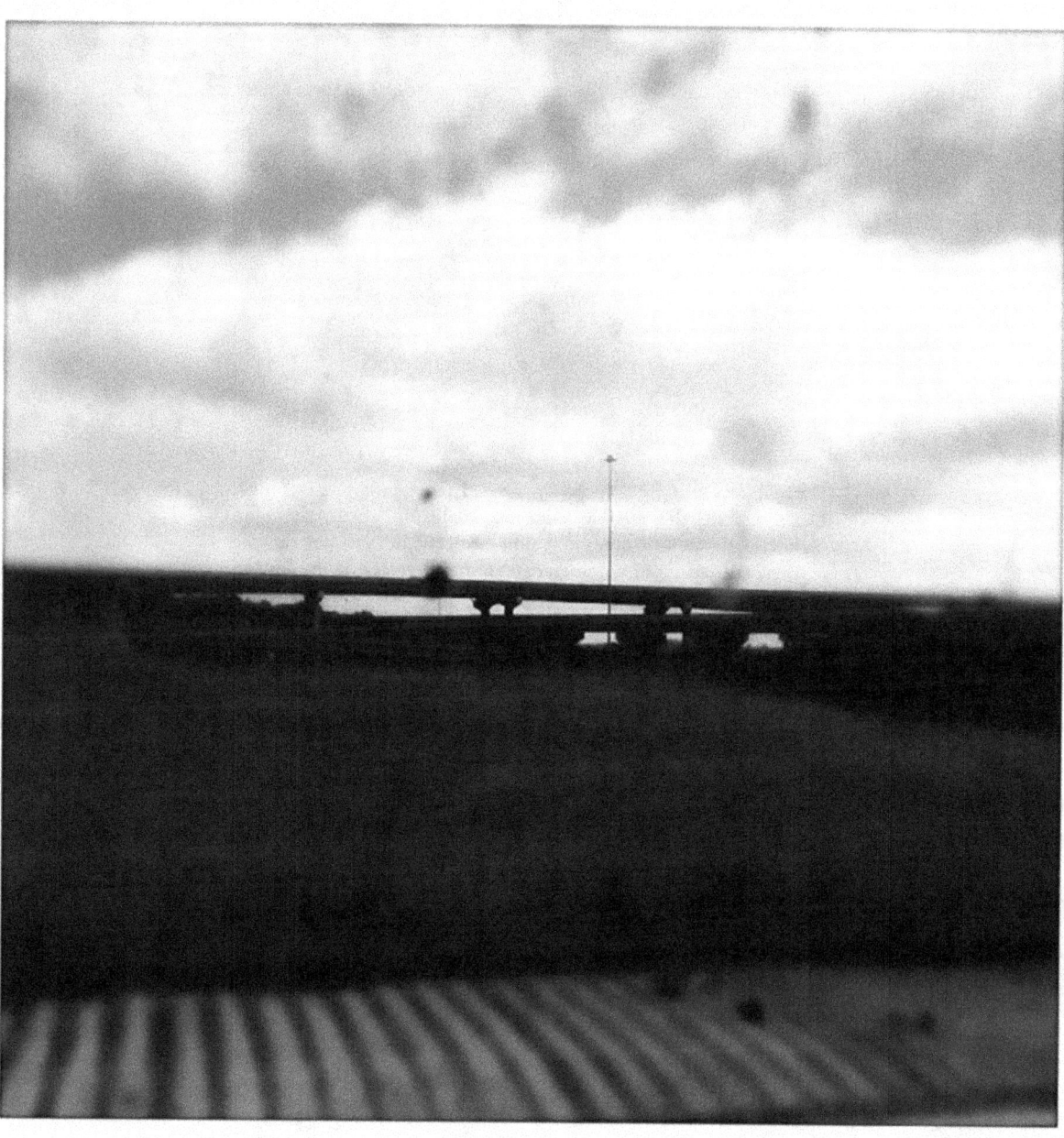

Drive, like a fledgling, to be free, felled to a landscape of muck. Desired mud, the terrible rains and delirium, drear, the road maker lays out his dredge. Think of it while you are at the market, the points of commerce, toxic herd, voices of the lowing in the rain thick gloom. When you are lost stop and listen for the hiss of tires, the gurgling toil of the tarmac resisting your fruits, your manure stained vegetables. Advance into the wail.

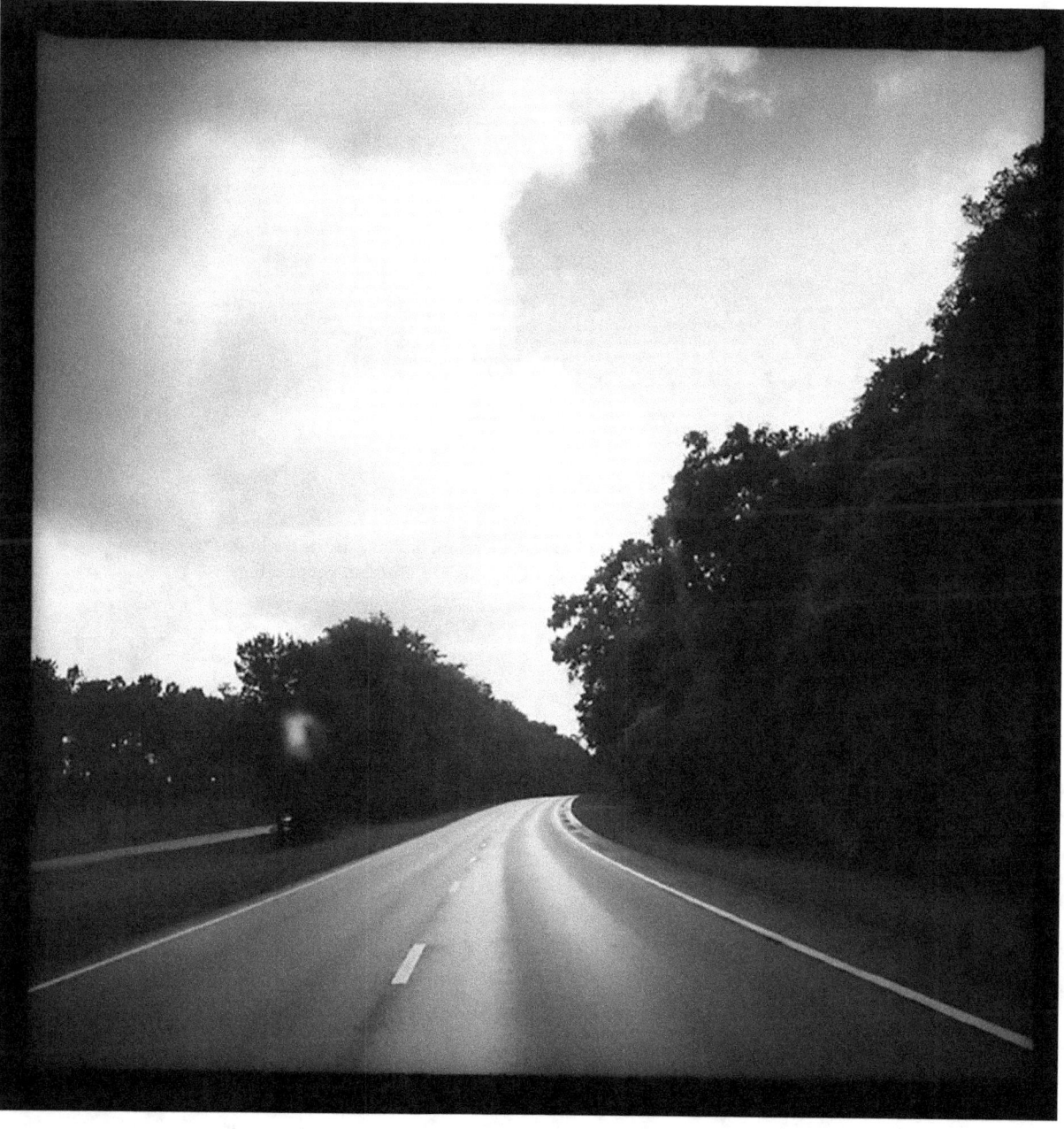

In these trees, the lolling heads of creation, bulbous hearts trailing fingers along the curved body of my creased horizon, penetrating.

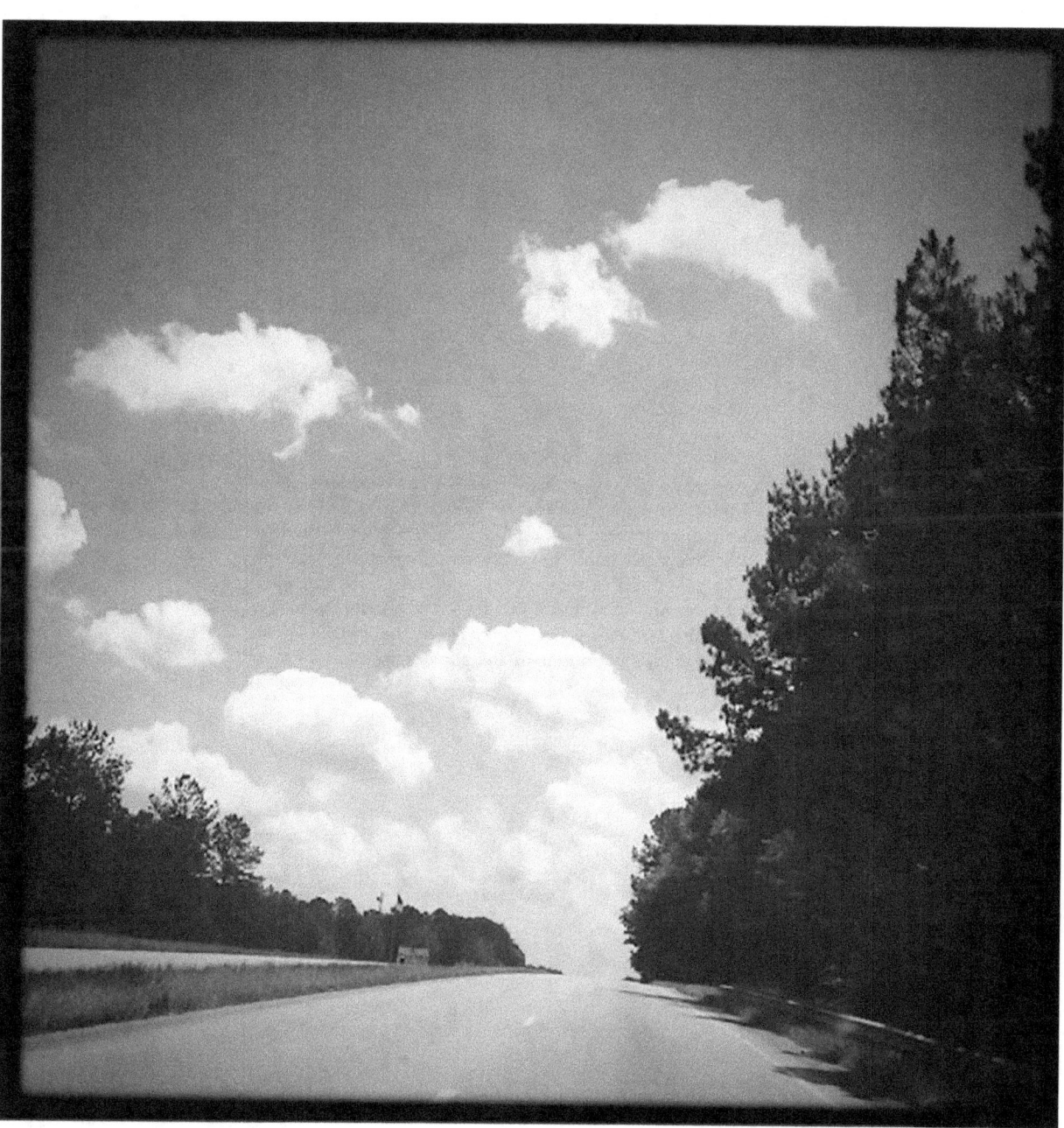

Here I am beneath these ruins, beneath this river, looking up. It was a costume party, extravagant unraveling. Cattle in the field, in their costumes, looking bored and agitated, ready to leave. But they don't know how, the door is missing suddenly. There is no gate but a cattle guard. I could stop here and watch them. Pull over on the roadside and let traffic hurtle, gnawing at the asphalt with tires. But I can't because of the invisible grate, how my foot could get caught in the slips of infinite darkness.

Then what, you might ask, looking down the road, away from the stalled vehicles, away from the fields of other people's work. You might have stayed, asked for a place at the edge, where the field surrenders to table tops. Is this perfection, you wonder, believing remotely in absolutes. You will set your foot in to a red ant mound and receive the world's response. There are only particulars. These random tiny pains and nowhere to run.

Holy church in the Gorgon's blood sprung from the quest for structure. I want to be a statue, with meaning to people who attend. Children will be bused to the museum to see me, my curly hair, standing out, and a surprised look, as when I am beheaded, or when I wake suddenly from drive-born meditation on collections, on arranging my shelves with plastic figurines of comic book characters, as when I was a child and thought I could be magically more than human and slightly beyond death, and I notice a the Honda in the left lane drifting perilous and gently into my lane and I am drawn in to a sudden world of legless fire. That moment the children will see and take photos of with their phones and text to each other that art is stupid and when is lunch.

Listen to your distant tears, take your stabilizer pills, the gears will shift to hold your engine to a resistant whine, in there, recline into the view of mesmerizing and ponderous herds of clouds, scattering to the cardinal east, always the tornadic east where the ghosts wave you on, recline.

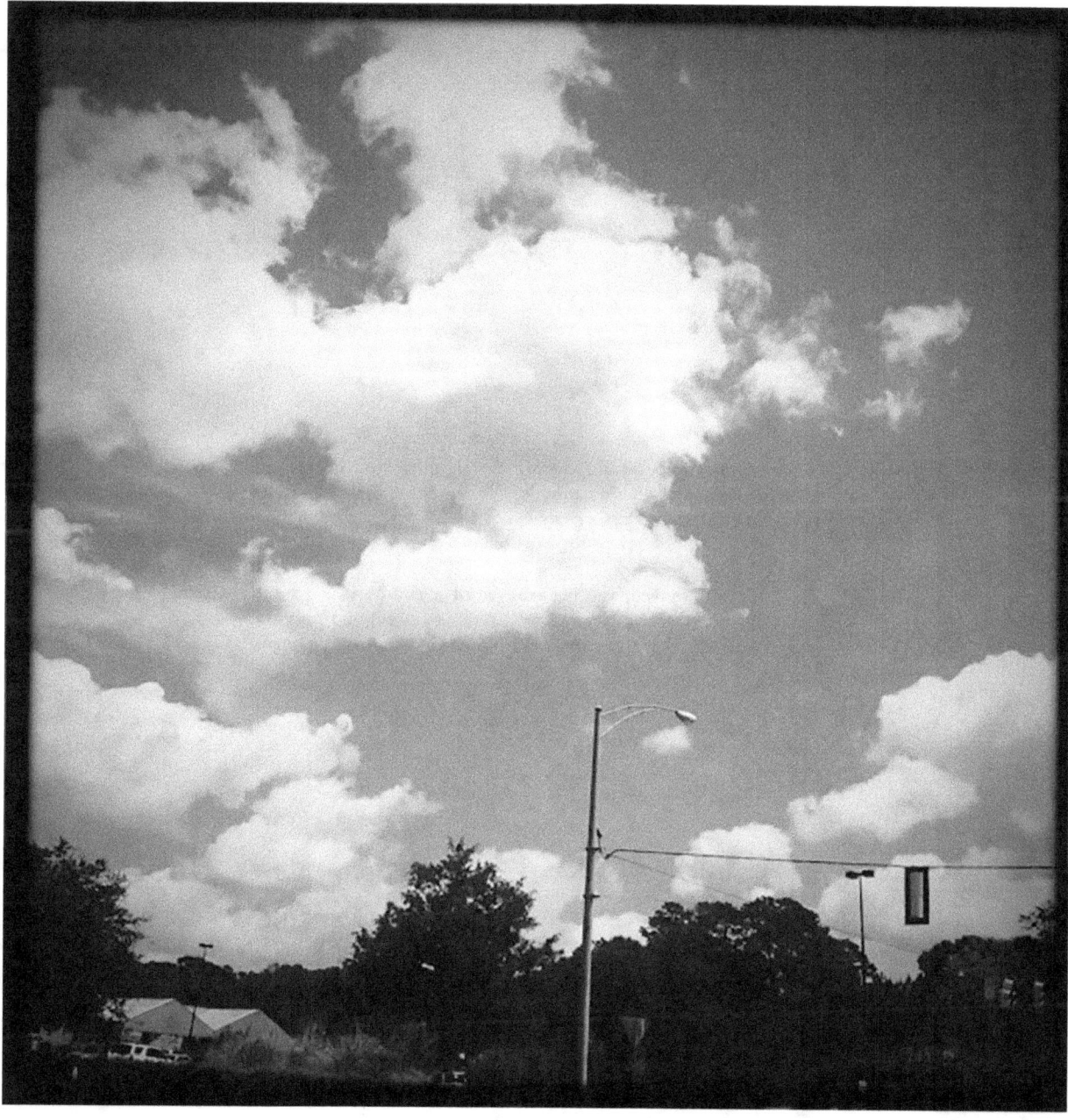

The descent in to bewilderment, the purging fire, begets the angelic, more and more meaningless, being more, more and more being, lifting up. There is a groove in the pavement cut by the rim of a truck's tire. After they explode at 91psi, there is little left. They blast can kill a man standing next to it, if he's lucky. Afterward, the space is removed, the pressure as of a child and a parent, the protection, as of a tree and its roots, is erased, and only the jagged edge rolls over and over, cutting its line, writing its poem.

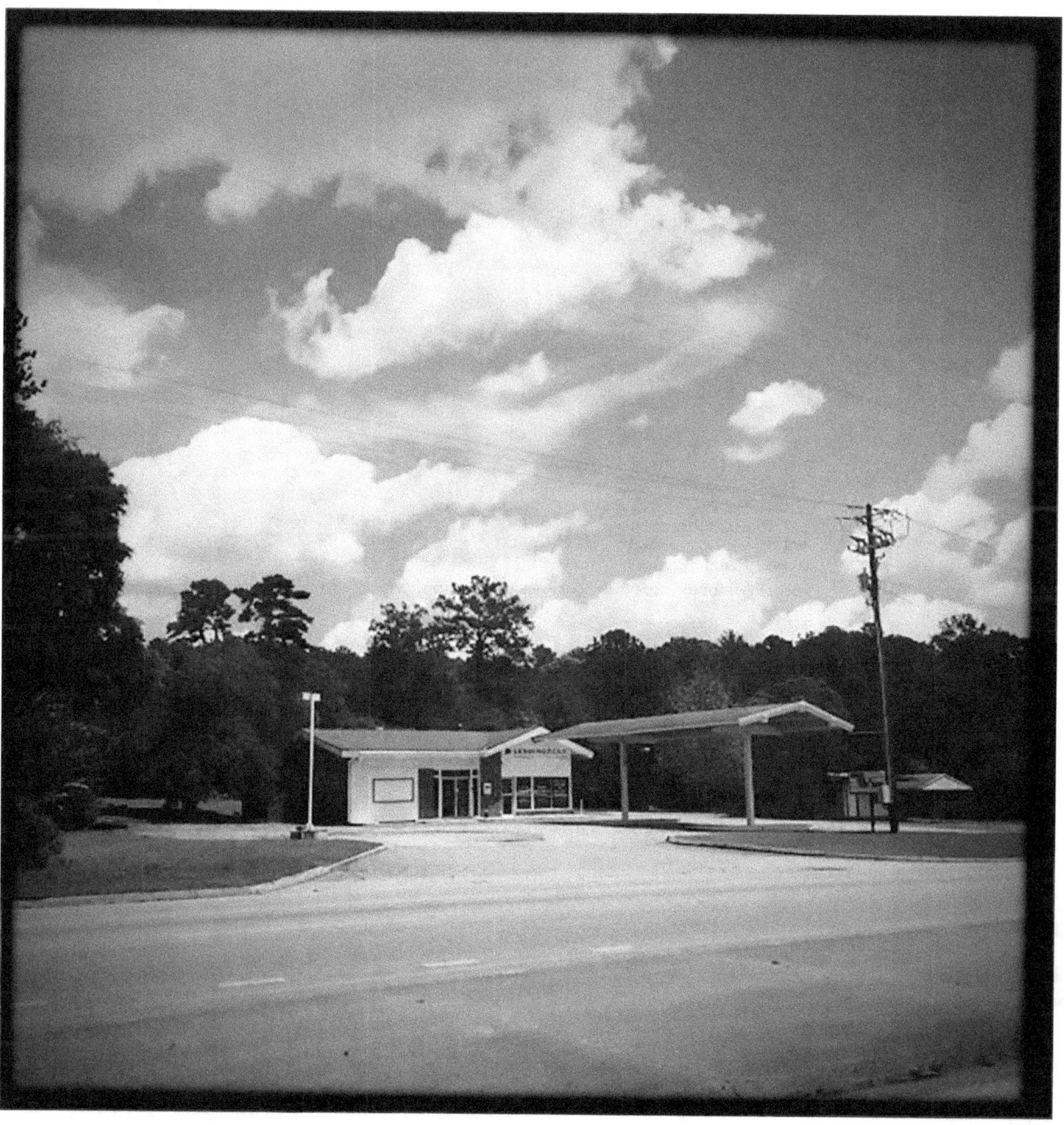

Lover of tulips, the temporary red buds in the maple, music that covers everything like light, the surrender into silence as in to water, submerged in scent.

No longer a perfect thing to be possessed, they hold it in possession, a gilded geometry to inspire. Instead, it is the propulsion, a wretched living as if gagged into being, vomited to life. Cut this here, the umbilical, the dangling treasure of Spanish moss sucking at the air and gently pulsing. No one knows how long the trip will be, how many hours. After a time, we stop asking, content to be in the air, above the torment of the ground.

Cascade of road, road of trees, of flowers and lowing creatures, of dark and crest, of blood and limit, grit and rubber, erosion, erosion interminable. Eat these sentences. Feed me the black top, the lines. Feed me the whole world.

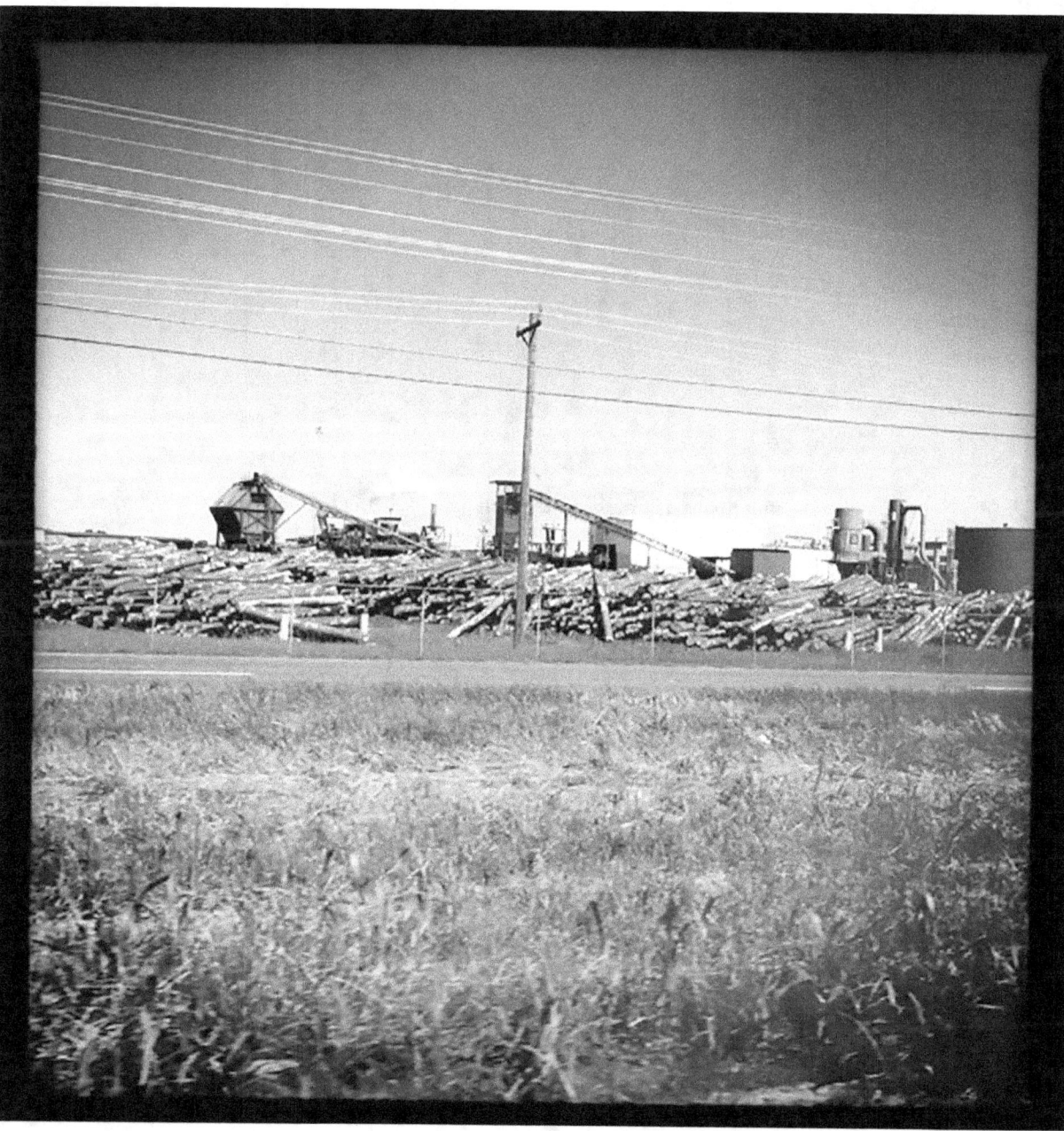

The air is troubled by the beneficent octopus, inked over to elude. A man occupies the yard in front of a mobile home. The grass is well tended beside the speed limit sign. Smoke from proscribed burning. One tree is burned almost all the way through. When it's done it will fall to make a home for the wind. There is no waving from the yard, not notice, possibly the finger, if anything, is given to no one cares.

Begging for love, shut your eyes so that only the lashes touch, keeping sand and whole visions at bay. Doubt these kisses, the rearview mirror knows nothing.

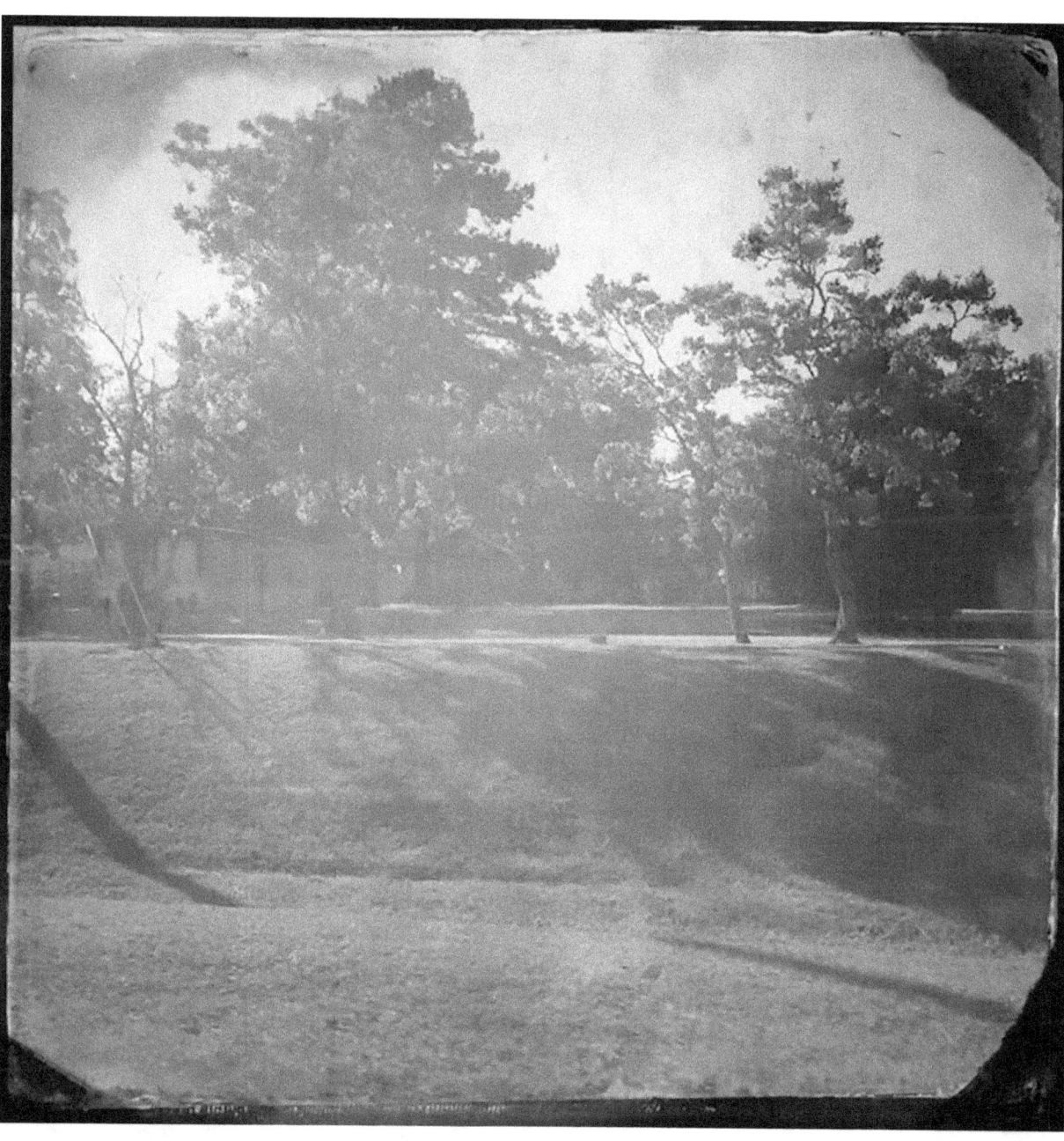

This road is swallowed by itself, by itself over again, one from the other. A serpent's tale. One horizon to the next, the same, really. Perhaps a patrol car is hiding in the thicket on this one. Perhaps it is the memory of ice cream. Either way, the side of the road must remain at the side. Not even a sign can cross over, unless the storm has come and carried it, yanking out the shadow and revealing a clutch of snakes.

Sinking into skunk smell, listing through hollows low with fog, cold pools of night air, audacity. Open the door and carry through.

You were a child, you were a road, you were a shadow. Former inhabitant lay in ruins. Ruin. The content of rain. The perpetual leveling, degrading.

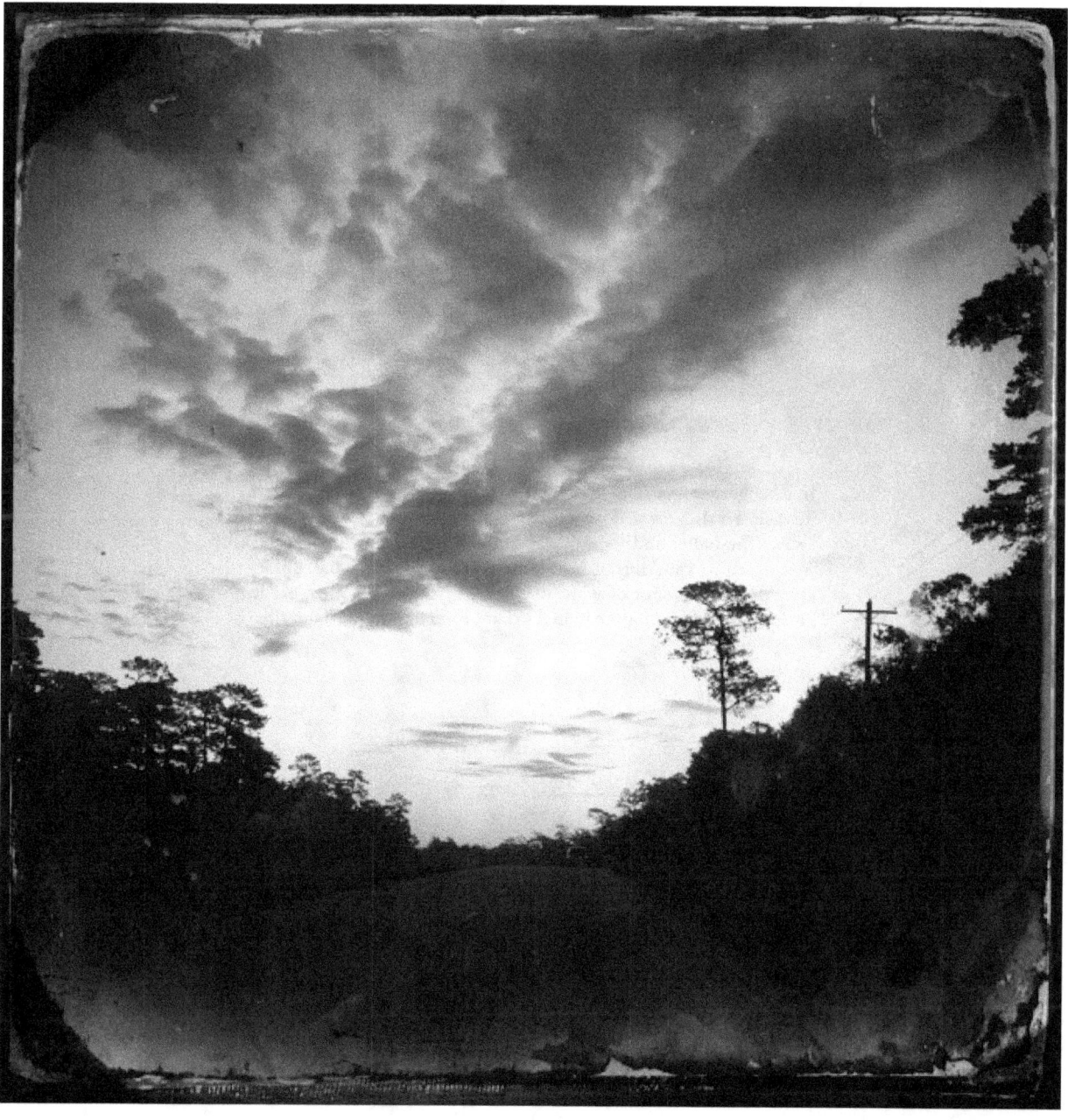

In the garden path a fledgling, dying, flaps helplessly. While further, a full grown dove pretends to be injured to entice you away. The ballet and its model. The dance of death, my brother would call it, thinking of how people are moved to small spasm after drinking a shot of whisky. The dove enticing you to eat it, performs her dance for the living. What prayer do you say if not this?

Sometimes I fall asleep and drift into the next century
where no one recognizes my car or my currency.

Also the spirit. Going on and on. Going. Laughter somewhere, and obsessions. Perpetual music. Playing into the peak, into the plummet. Sound out the cry for help, the cry.

This road, dark ray from a dark sun, caught, beam.

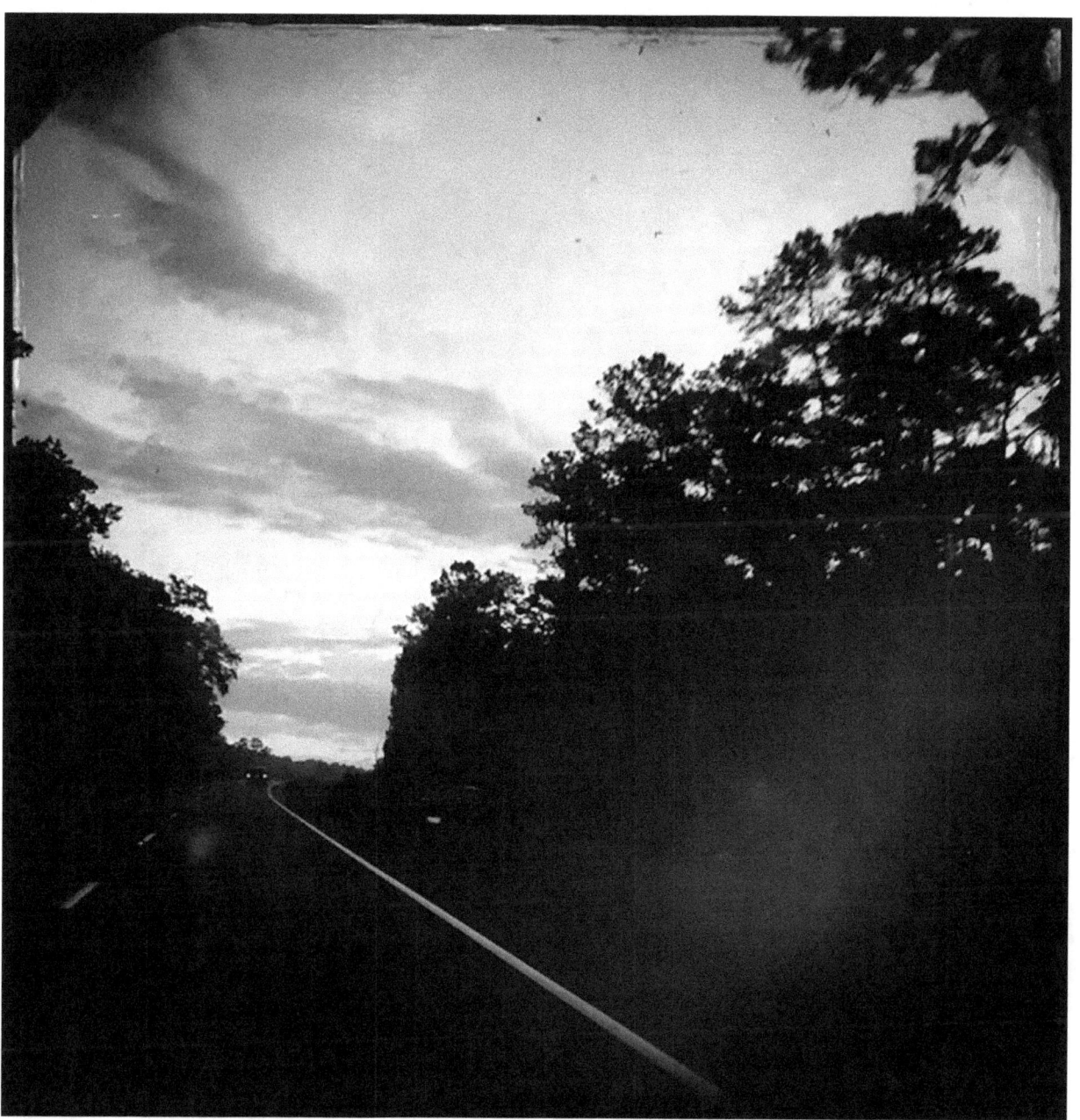

Needle injecting sunlight, needle injecting road. In the exam room I lift one arm, then the other. I've taken the day off from driving to drive to the doctor's. It's early and my head hurts from interrupting my pattern. I think of bees examining alfalfa blossoms, maybe in the manicured hedge right in front of the doctor's building. I could never afford this life. I should have been a tea bush groomed to be decorative. I should have been a chamber made to echo wind. Cicada's grind themselves out of their shells. I am drowsy in the sunlight on the paper sheet. The paper comes from a spool, I write my germs on it. When I am gone they will tear it off and unravel some more. Another road to crease.

The wrecker's cross. Hangs up the monument of wreck and cloud. Of crying moments, for forgetting.

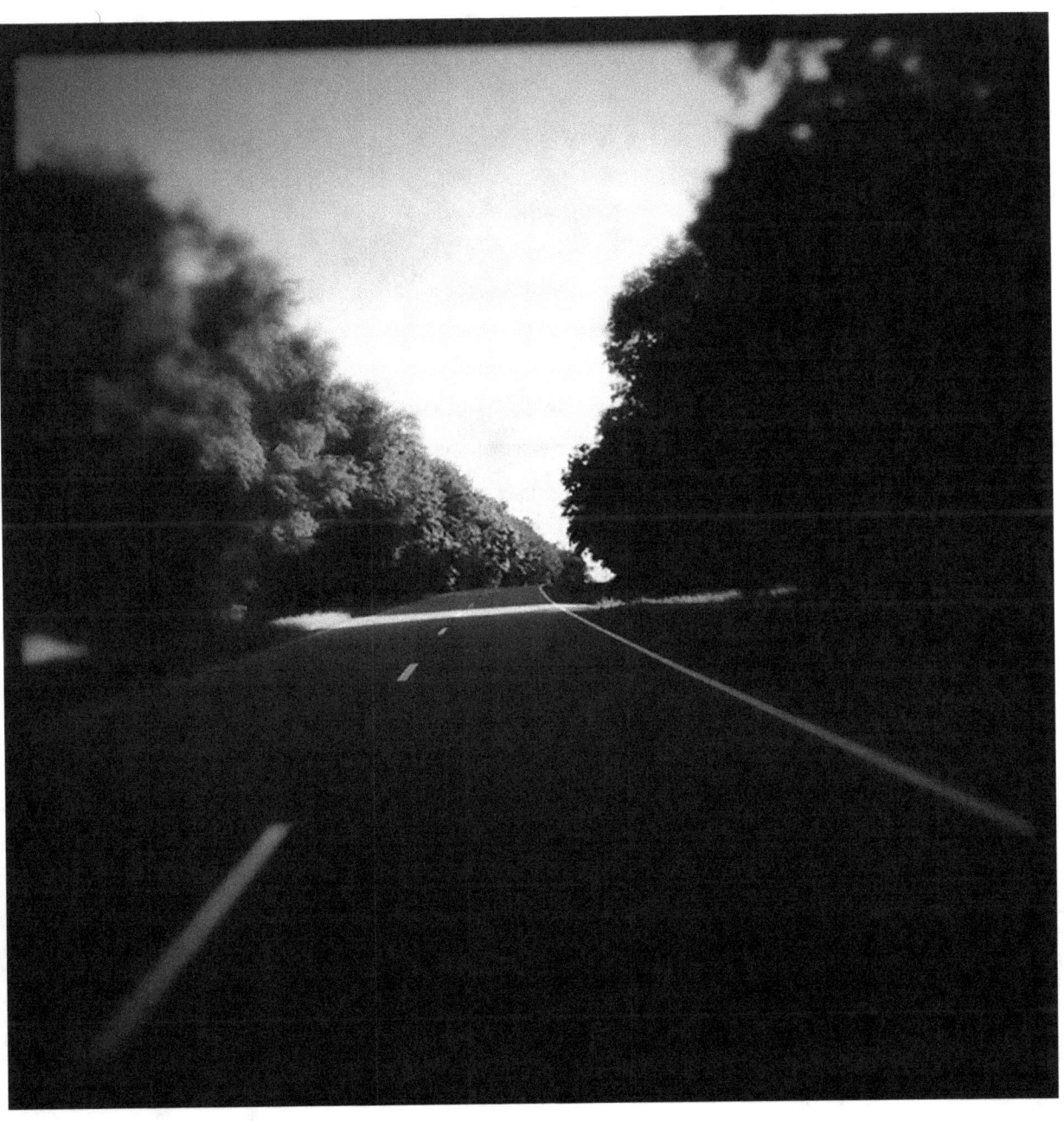

This is a seam in the monument, moniker of earth, evidence of the hue and weight of time, look up. The statue is forlorn. War man, suffering woman. Horse, noble in service. I have a car. It's nice. I drive it. The road bends, switches surface according to tax base. Sometimes the cracks are closed in with a dark glue. It makes a rhythm on the tires. When I get home there are tar streaks on the door, there are insect remains on the windshield. Municipalities put statues at the center of things as though anyone would drive slow enough to observe. Replacing art with commerce, the center of every town is the Dollar General. The home church.

Some wake to apparitions, others to tractor trailers, either the return of sky to the horizon or the seam unveiling. I'm alive in this, almost despairing, rub of trees, of burnt grass in the swale, I am arisen to horizon.

Night blooming flowers, nightshades, tomatoes and tobacco, finger direct witch finger leaves pointing at you, clawing indication, yellow flasher, yellow flasher, your whole life an occasion.

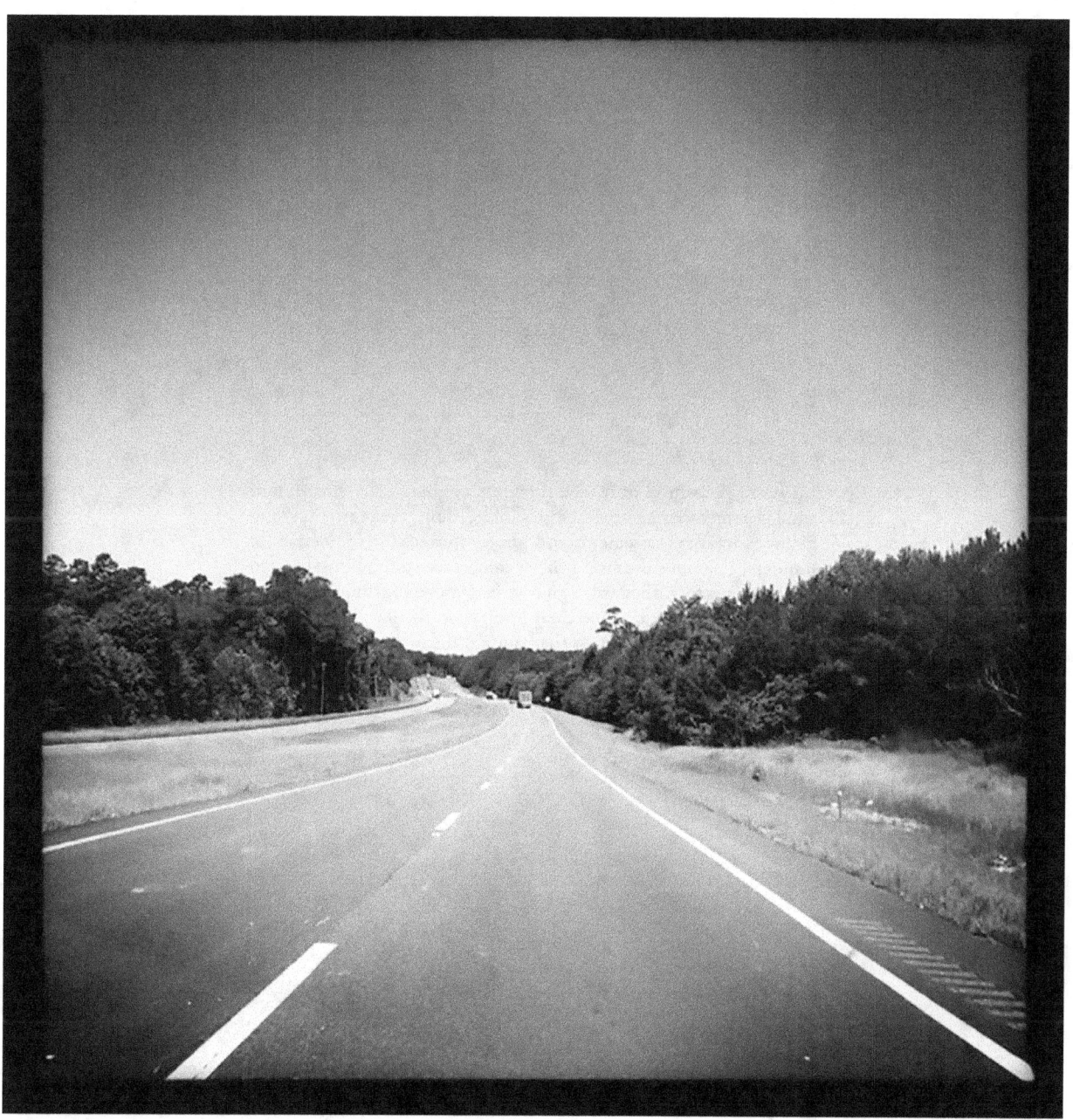

Listen to the sound of wheel, lurching, engine's close breath and wind, I remember the priests in parade, along the way. They had balloons in silver casement, and plastic flowers for the occasion. Banners, a parade. The emergency vehicles are so bright we have to close our eyes to it. They are so loud we look away. The caravan of faces in the distance look up from their interests and know the sounds of night birds will return. Birds that contain the night. The ministers.

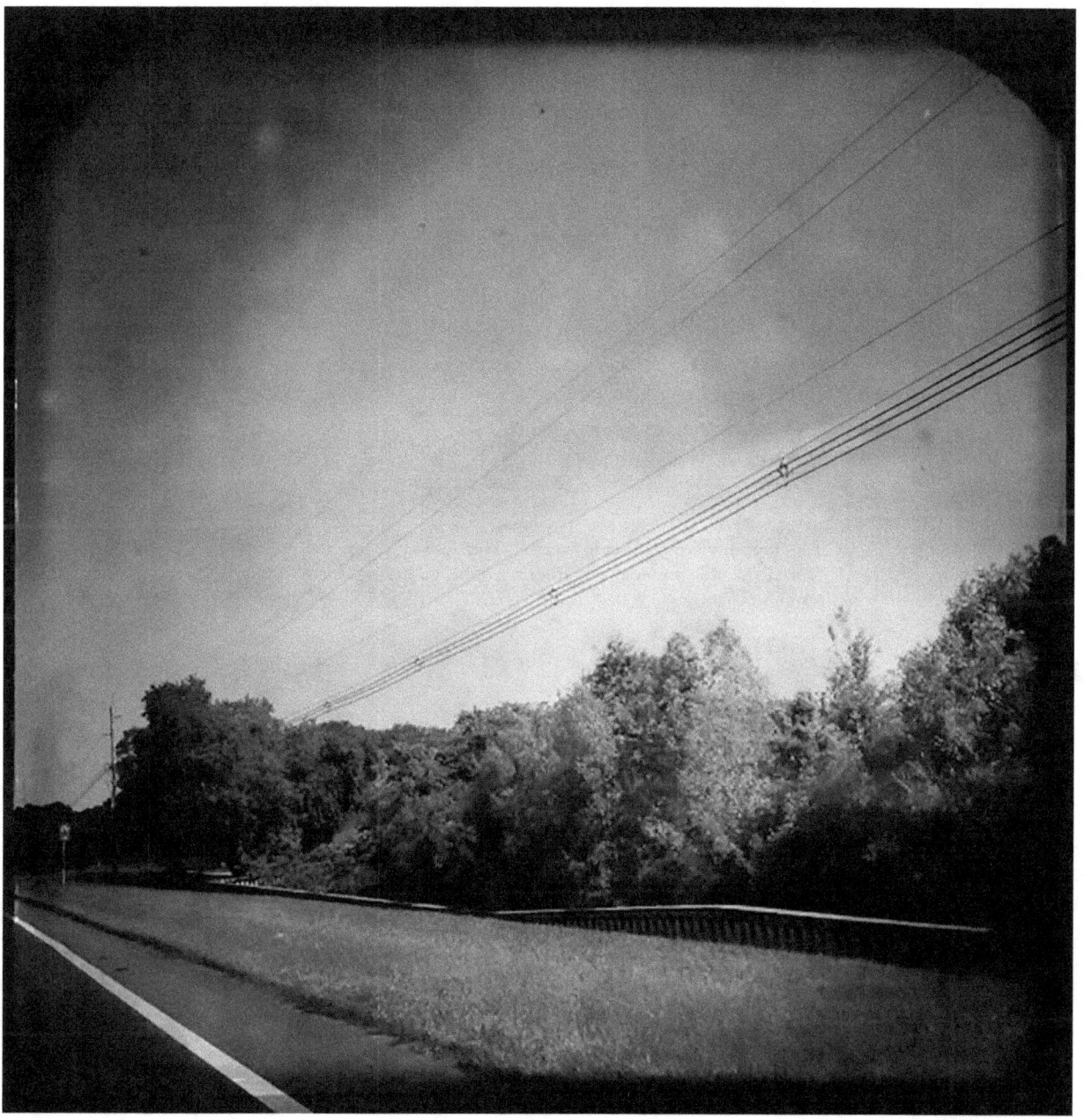

The moon also is a cold vessel. Her blood drips the jailer's footfalls. Cold in predawn, gathering light, gathering dread. Sighs.

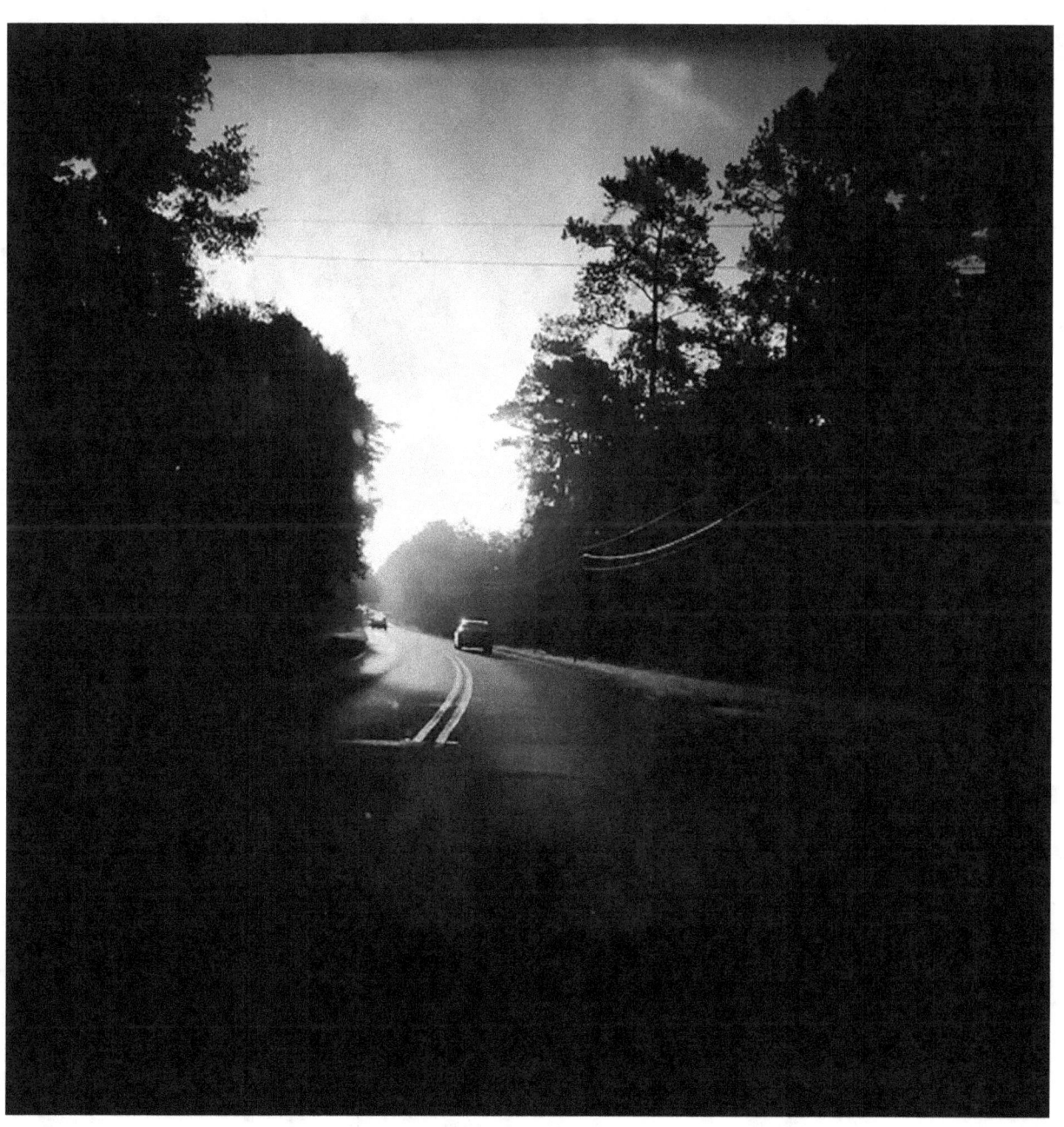

I see you also, back on the bank, the submerged. I am safe in the water. Drowned in a burnished sky. The road is the color of knowing. North road, secret door, peeling away the bark, revealing cold light. South Road, gateway of dust, rising particles and exhalation. Only the sun makes the shadow road. No other passage is possible. I make a cocktail at the drinks table and pretend that I can speak. I am submerged in this voiclessness for as long as there are shadows. As long as it takes for you to arrive.

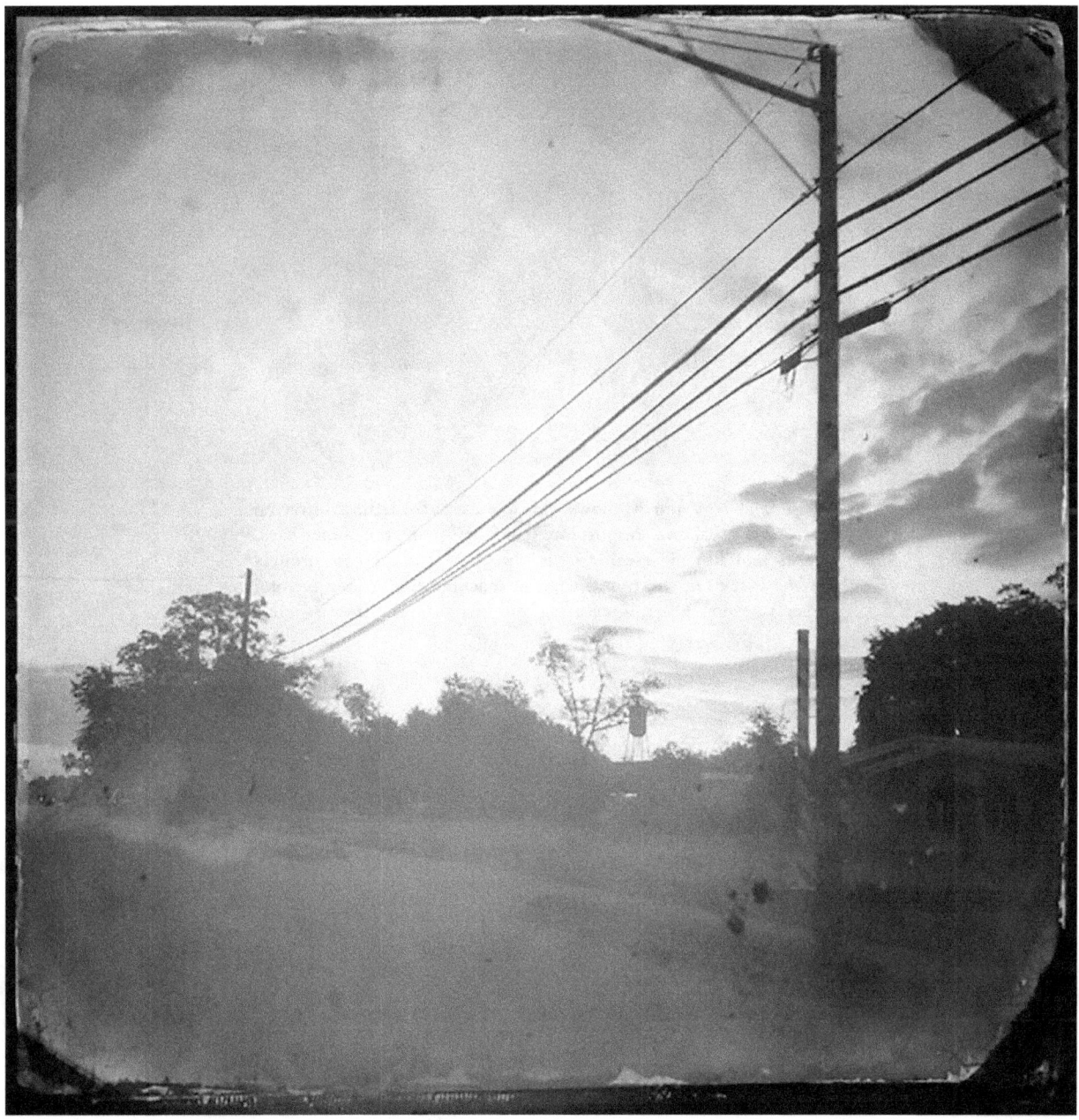

A duty of legs and windows. An age of self-worth. a hurrying into the escalator, important meetings with the pine bark, flakes and hot air escaping the throat of the air conditioners in the black tar, the tarred edge of machine life, grease turning wheels, your heart greased into turning one more trick.

Pity road, pity slurry, pity the distended, pity somnambulant, pity the engine forced into fire, pity the burning look, the visage of gambler's sky, of lunatic fury, pity failure. Pity the robot's intention to interpret, the box with a face, the car with eyes, the ribbon tying shut the gift of days, the passage, the passer. Pity the walker, observing, Pity the sad angry, pity the cloud, her tears, pity the turn, made.

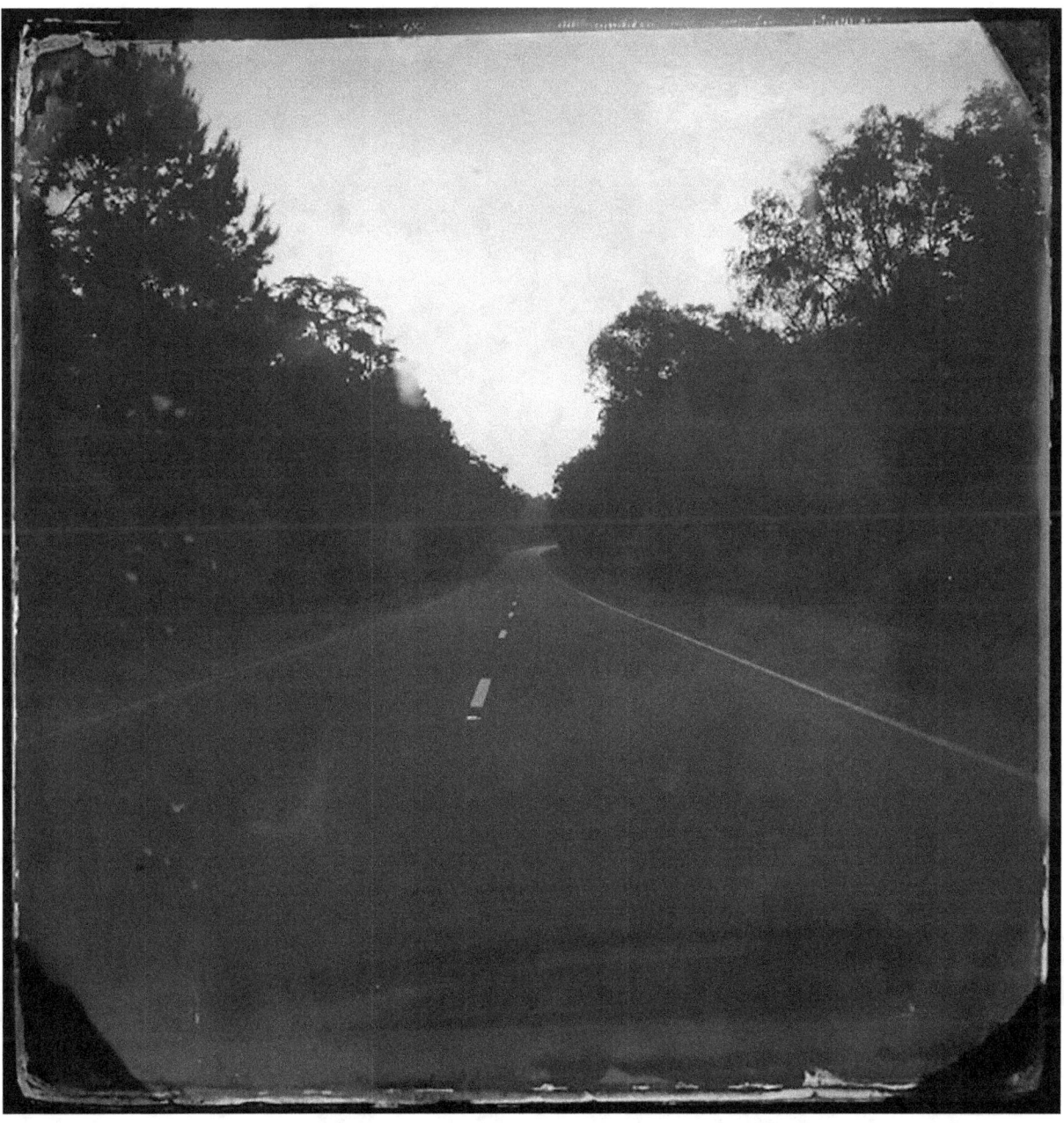

The road keeps what you cannot. It bends but is never hobbled. It buckles but never gives you away. I am drowned in the dark river. I have always been here, driving. If you look down you can see me, monument eyes. If you look down you will fall into me. I will not be set free.

Roses are heavy, they cost arms and loads and gallons of jet fuel. They cost hearts and party favors and whole purchased homes. I love the carriage and the body transported. I love the spring of streetlights abruptly becoming an orange night. I love the dusk, its sweet taking, its pity. I am an exile, too. Exile to you, with you, within. I can provide the dark and the movement. And perhaps the language.

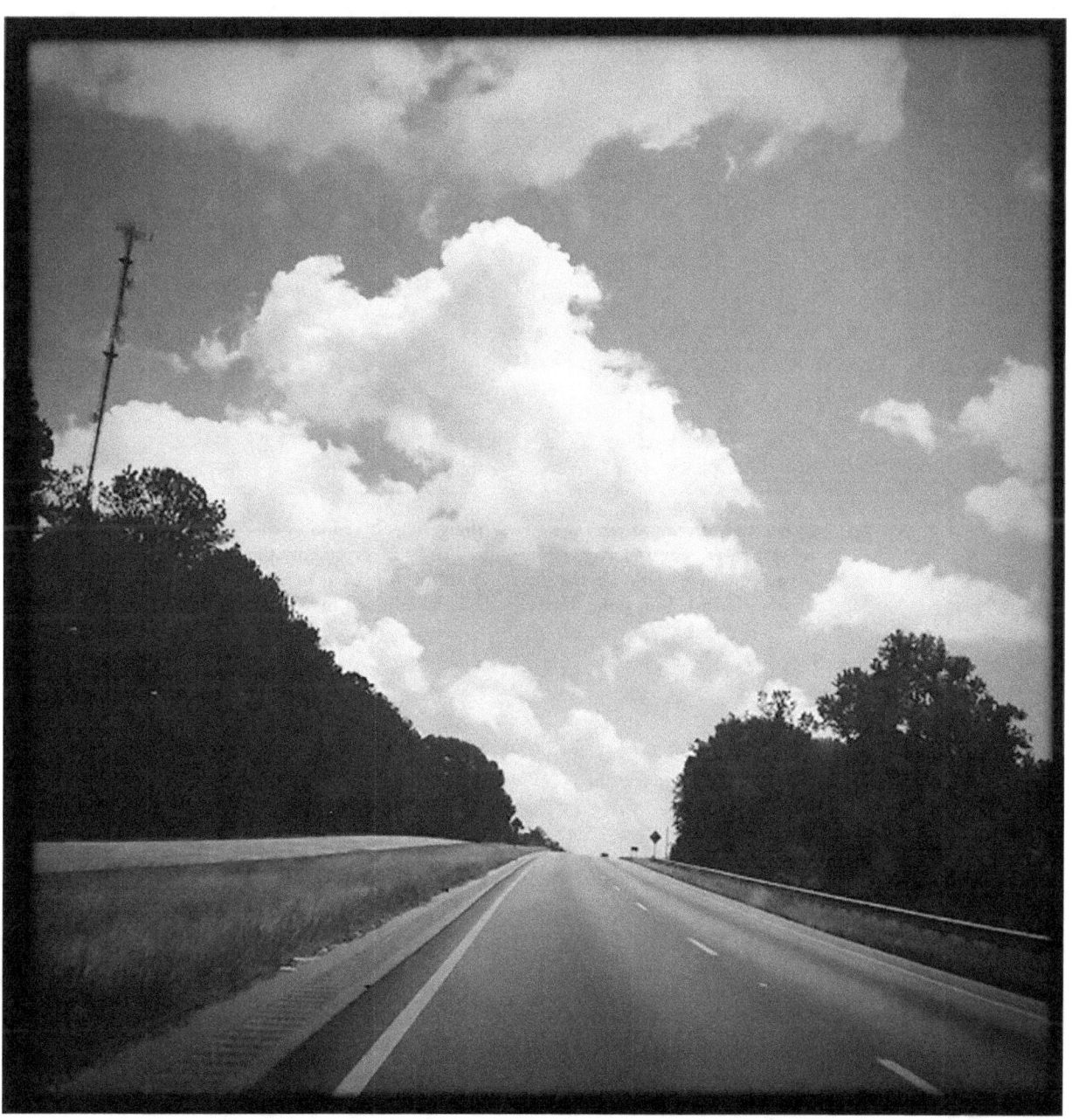

Pearls and offering, I am seeing well, the goodness , round gems in your eyes, entertaining. There are shards of crystal in the pavement. They sparkle in the sun. They stride always out in front of you, like a ball of light. If you go fast enough, you may enter.

I have nothing really to give so you should take all you can.

www.ingramcontent.com/pod-product-compliance
Lightning Source LLC
Chambersburg PA
CBHW080806180526
45168CB00006B/2344